HOME & AWAY

HOME&AWAY

Knits *for* Everyday Adventures

HANNAH FETTIG

PHOTOGRAPHS BY DANIEL HUDSON

ISBN 978-0-692-36816-9
First Edition

Graphic design by Mary Joy Gumayagay
Printed in the United States by Puritan Press

Back River Bend, Georgetown, Maine

For knitters *and* adventurers.

CONTENTS

INTRODUCTION

Early mornings building a fire. Making coffee. Reading. A glass of wine during dinner preparations. A post-dinner family dance party. Playgrounds. Tide pools. Farmers markets. Snowmen. At this stage in my life, with two small children at home, it is all about the everyday adventures. I keep my wardrobe pretty minimal, with 3–5 outfits in high rotation. As time marches on I move closer and closer to a uniform that will be worn every day, though I'd like to think I'll always want at least a little variety!

In these pages you will find knits that will become wardrobe essentials—nothing ornate or precious, but pieces with simple lines knit in wonderful, well-wearing wool.

Since 2009 I've designed many top down raglan sweaters with not a seam in sight. More recently I've been reminded of the benefits of seams. And so we have two camps: those who choose to seam and those who prefer to not. Well, good news for all: for each top down seamless raglan pattern in this book, instructions are also included to knit the sweater in pieces from the bottom up and then seam them. You can choose your own adventure! Either way you'll end up with the same result.

A year ago Pam Allen (my knitting hero) and I started a podcast called *knit.fm*. Our goal for the podcast was to help people become better knitters. It definitely helped me grow as a knitter—I learned from Pam, our guest hosts, and all the interesting questions and feedback we got from listeners. Much of the extra content you'll find in this book was inspired by *knit.fm*: discussions on gauge, fit, understanding a knitting pattern, and more.

May this book serve you both practically and inspirationally—to dream, plan and knit! I dedicate this one to you knitters.

Hannah
Portland, Maine
March 25, 2015

LET'S CONNECT!

FIND a *Ravelry* coupon code, on the inside back cover of this book, good for one digital copy of *Home & Away*. If you aren't familiar with *Ravelry*, it's an invaluable website where the online knitting community gathers. Millions of users swap information on patterns, yarns, techniques and inspiration. You'll no doubt spend a lot of time online at

www.ravelry.com

JOIN the *Home & Away* group on *Ravelry* to connect with other knitters working on projects from the book!

www.ravelry.com/groups/home-and-away

SHARE your knitting progress and finished projects on *Instagram* and *Twitter* with the hashtag #knitbot on

www.instagram.com/knitbot
www. twitter.com/hannahfettig

WATCH for additional *Home & Away* content, including finished project galleries, on

www.knitbot.com

QUESTIONS about a pattern? Check in with the *Ravelry* group or send an e-mail to

info@knitbot.com

ERRATA for all patterns are available on our website

www.knitbot.com/errata

PLANTS
Stories of
Legendary
Heroes

GEORGETOWN

Is it possible to have a sweater be both tailored and effortless? Georgetown *says yes, with a comfortable open fit and wide, folded-over collar. Knitted in a cozy wool / alpaca woolen spun yarn, you will want to curl up in your nook with a favorite book.*

The pictured sweater was knitted flat in pieces. In the first set of instructions the body, fronts, and sleeves are worked separately and seamed together. If you prefer seamless knitting, instructions follow for a mostly seamless cardigan. In this version the back and sides are knit simultaneously from the bottom up. Divide for armholes, knit the fronts and back separately, and seam the shoulders. The sleeves are then knitted from the top down using short rows.

FINISHED MEASUREMENTS
Chest circumference: 30.5 (34.5, 38.5, 42.5, 46.5)[50.5, 54.5, 58.5, 62.5]" / 77 (87.5, 97.5, 107.5, 118)[128, 138, 148.5, 158.5] cm
Shown in size 34.5" / 87.5 cm with 2" / 5 cm of positive ease.

YARN
10 (11, 12, 13, 14)[15, 17, 18, 19] skeins Quince & Co. *Owl* (50% American wool, 50% American alpaca; 120 yd / 110 m per 50 g skein) in Abyssinian

OR 1100 (1250, 1375, 1500, 1675)[1800, 1950, 2100, 2275] yd / 1000 (1125, 1250, 1375, 1525)[1650, 1775, 1925, 2075] m of worsted weight yarn

NEEDLES
US 7 / 4.5 mm:
- 32" / 80 cm circular needle

US 5 / 3.75 mm:
- 32" / 80 cm circular needle

Or size needed to obtain gauge.

NOTIONS
Stitch markers, stitch holders or waste yarn, tapestry needle

GAUGE
20 sts and 28 rows = 4" / 10 cm in St st on larger needles

KNIT IN PIECES AND SEAMED

BACK
With smaller circular needle and using a long-tail cast on, CO 80 (90, 100, 110, 120)[130, 140, 150, 160] sts.

RIBBING SETUP ROW (RS): (K1, p1) rep to end.

Cont in ribbing as est for 12 rows more, ending with a RS row.

Switch to larger needle.

Purl 1 WS row.

DEC ROW (RS): K2, ssk, knit to last 4 sts, k2tog, k2. 2 sts dec.

Cont in St st, rep this dec row every 12 rows 4 times more. 70 (80, 90, 100, 110)[120, 130, 140, 150] sts.

Cont in St st for 7 rows, ending with a WS row.

INC ROW (RS): K2, M1L, knit to last 2 sts, M1R, k2. 2 sts inc.

Rep this inc row every 18th row twice more. 76 (86, 96, 106, 116)[126, 136, 146, 156] sts.

Cont in St st until body meas 16.5 (17, 17.5, 18, 18.5)[19, 19.5, 20, 20.5]" / 42 (43, 44.5, 45.5, 47)[48.5, 49.5, 51, 52] cm or desired length, ending with a WS row.

SHAPE ARMHOLE
BO 3 (5, 6, 8, 9)[11, 12, 14, 15] sts at beg of next 2 rows. 70 (76, 84, 90, 98)[104, 112, 118, 126] sts.

DEC ROW (RS): K2, ssk, knit to last 4 sts, k2tog, k2. 2 sts dec.

Rep this dec row every RS row 1 (1, 4, 7, 9)[11, 13, 15, 17] time(s) more, then every 4th row 1 (2, 1, 0, 0)[0, 0, 0, 0] time(s) more. 64 (68, 72, 74, 78)[80, 84, 86, 90] sts.

Cont in St st until armhole meas 6.5 (7, 7.5, 8, 8.5)[9, 9.5, 10, 10.5]" / 16.5 (18, 19, 20.5, 21.5)[23, 24, 25.5, 26.5) cm, ending with a WS row.

SHAPE SHOULDERS
BO 7 (7, 8, 8, 9)[9, 10, 10, 11] sts at beg of next 2 rows, then BO 7 (8, 8, 9, 9)[10, 10, 11, 11] sts at beg of next 2 rows. BO 36 (38, 40, 40, 42)[42, 44, 44, 46] rem back neck sts.

LEFT FRONT
With smaller circular needle and using a long-tail cast on, CO 22 (26, 30, 35, 39)[44, 48, 53, 57] sts.

SIZES 42.5, 46.5, 58.5 AND 62.5" / 107.5, 118, 148.5 AND 158.5 CM ONLY
RIBBING SETUP ROW (RS): (P1, k1) rep to last st, p1.

SIZES 30.5, 34.5, 38.5, 50.5 AND 54.5" / 77, 87.5, 97.5, 128 AND 138 CM ONLY
RIBBING SETUP ROW (RS): (K1, p1) rep to end.

ALL SIZES
Cont in ribbing as est for 12 rows more, ending with a RS row.

Switch to larger needle.

Purl 1 WS row.

DEC ROW (RS): K2, ssk, knit to end. 1 st dec.

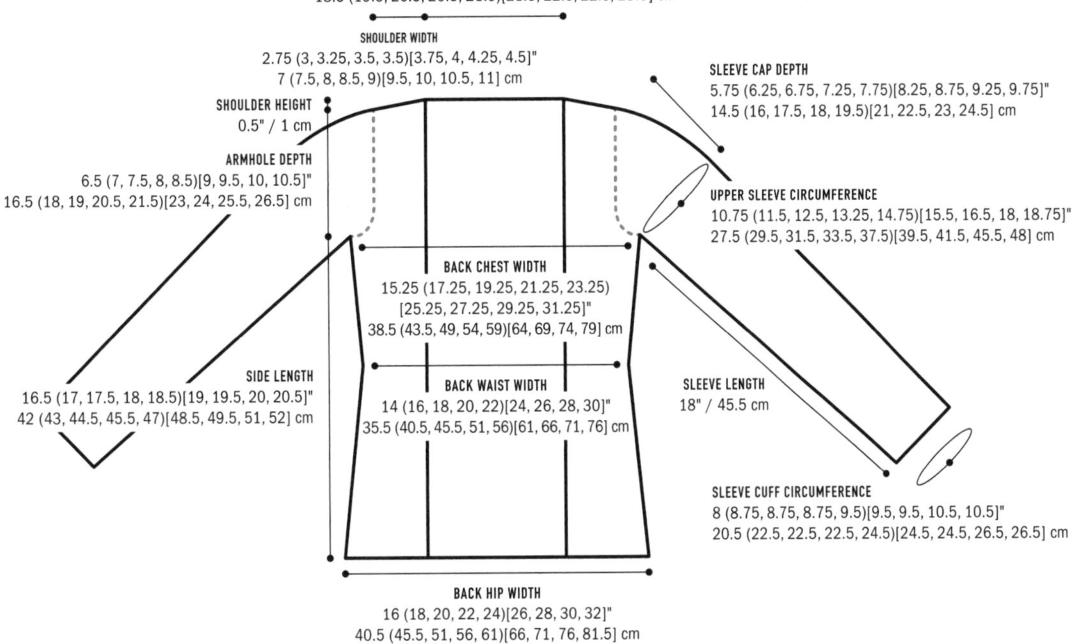

Cont in St st, rep this dec row every 12 rows 4 times more. 17 (21, 25, 30, 34)[39, 43, 48, 52] sts.

Cont in St st for 7 rows, ending with a WS row.

INC ROW (RS): K2, M1L, knit to end. 1 st inc.

Rep this inc row every 18th row twice more. 20 (24, 28, 33, 37)[42, 46, 51, 55] sts.

Cont in St st until body matches length of back, ending with a WS row.

SHAPE ARMHOLE

BO 3 (5, 6, 8, 9)[11, 12, 14, 15] sts, knit to end. 17 (19, 22, 25, 28)[31, 34, 37, 40] sts.

Purl 1 WS row.

DEC ROW (RS): K2, ssk, knit to end. 1 st dec.

Rep this dec row every RS row 1 (1, 4, 7, 9)[11, 13, 15, 17] time(s) more, then every 4th row 1 (2, 1, 0, 0)[0, 0, 0, 0] time(s) more. 14 (15, 16, 17, 18)[19, 20, 21, 22] sts.

Cont in St st until armhole matches length of back armhole, ending with a WS row.

SHAPE SHOULDER

BO 7 (7, 8, 8, 9)[9, 10, 10, 11] sts, knit to end.

Purl 1 WS row.

BO rem 7 (8, 8, 9, 9)[10, 10, 11, 11] sts.

RIGHT FRONT

With smaller circular needle and using a long-tail cast on, CO 22 (26, 30, 35, 39)[44, 48, 53, 57] sts.

SIZES 42.5, 46.5, 58.5 AND 62.5" / 107.5, 118, 148.5 AND 158.5 CM ONLY

RIBBING SETUP ROW (RS): P1, (k1, p1) rep to end.

SIZES 30.5, 34.5, 38.5, 50.5 AND 54.5" / 77, 87.5, 97.5, 128 AND 138 CM ONLY

RIBBING SETUP ROW (RS): (K1, p1) rep to end.

ALL SIZES

Cont in ribbing as est for 12 rows more, ending with a RS row.

Switch to larger needle.

Purl 1 WS row.

DEC ROW (RS): Knit to last 4 sts, k2tog, k2. 1 st dec.

Cont in St st, rep this dec row every 12 rows 4 times more. 17 (21, 25, 30, 34)[39, 43, 48, 52] sts.

Cont in St st for 7 rows, ending with a WS row.

INC ROW (RS): Knit to last 2 sts, M1R, k2. 1 st inc.

Rep this inc row every 18th row twice more. 20 (24, 28, 33, 37)[42, 46, 51, 55] sts.

Cont in St st until body matches length of back, ending with a RS row.

SHAPE ARMHOLE

BO 3 (5, 6, 8, 9)[11, 12, 14, 15] sts, purl to end. 17 (19, 22, 25, 28)[31, 34, 37, 40] sts.

DEC ROW (RS): Knit to last 4 sts, k2tog, k2. 1 st dec.

Rep this dec row every RS row 1 (1, 4, 7, 9)[11, 13, 15, 17] time(s) more, then every 4th row 1 (2, 1, 0, 0)[0, 0, 0, 0] time(s) more. 14 (15, 16, 17, 18)[19, 20, 21, 22] sts.

Cont in St st until armhole matches length of back armhole, ending with a RS row.

SHAPE SHOULDER

BO 7 (7, 8, 8, 9)[9, 10, 10, 11] sts, purl to end.

Knit 1 RS row.

BO rem 7 (8, 8, 9, 9)[10, 10, 11, 11] sts.

SLEEVES
With smaller needle, CO 40 (44, 44, 44, 48)[48, 48, 52, 52] sts.

RIBBING SETUP ROW (RS): (K1, p1) rep to end.

Cont in ribbing as est for 4" / 10 cm, ending with a RS row.

Switch to larger needle.

Purl 1 WS row.

INC ROW (RS): K2, M1L, knit to last 2 sts, M1R, k2. 2 sts inc.

Cont in St st, rep this inc row every 14 (14, 12, 10, 8)[6, 6, 6, 6] rows 6 (6, 2, 2, 6)[14, 10, 6, 2] times more, then every 0 (0, 10, 8, 6)[0, 4, 4, 4] rows 0 (0, 6, 8, 6)[0, 6, 12, 18] times more. 54 (58, 62, 66, 74)[78, 82, 90, 94] sts.

Cont in St st until sleeve meas 18" / 45.5 cm or desired length, ending with a WS row.

SHAPE CAP
BO 3 (5, 6, 8, 9)[11, 12, 14, 15] sts at beg of next 2 rows. 48 (48, 50, 50, 56)[56, 58, 62, 64] sts.

DEC ROW (RS): K2, ssk, knit to last 4 sts, k2tog, k2. 2 sts dec.

Rep dec row every RS row 1 (1, 1, 1, 3)[2, 2, 4, 4] time(s) more, then rep dec row every 4th row 3 (5, 6, 7, 6)[8, 9, 8, 9] times more, then rep dec row every RS row 8 (6, 6, 5, 7)[6, 6, 7, 7] times more. 22 sts.

Purl 1 WS row.

DEC ROW 1 (RS): K2, ssk, knit to last 4 sts, k2tog, k2. 2 sts dec.
DEC ROW 2 (WS): P2, ssp, purl to last 4 sts, p2tog, p2. 2 sts dec.

Rep the last 2 dec rows 2 times more. 10 sts.

BO rem 10 sts.

FINISHING
Sew shoulder seams.

COLLAR
Using smaller needles and beg at the bottom right edge, pick up and knit 2 sts for every 3 rows up the right front of the cardigan, pick up and knit 37 (39, 41, 41, 43)[43, 45, 45, 47] sts evenly across back neck, then pick up and knit 2 sts for every 3 rows down the left front. Your final st count should be an odd number.

RIBBING SETUP ROW (WS): (K1, p1) rep to last st, k1.

Cont in ribbing as est for 4" / 10 cm.

Switch to larger needle.

Cont in ribbing until collar meas 7.75 (8, 8.5, 8.5, 9)[9, 9.25, 9.25, 9.75]" / 19.5 (20.5, 21.5, 21.5, 22.5)[22.5, 23.5, 23.5, 24.5] cm.

BO loosely in ribbing.

Sew sleeve cap into armhole. Sew sleeve and side seams.

Weave in all ends. Block to measurements.

KNIT MOSTLY SEAMLESS

BODY
With smaller circular needle and using a long-tail cast on, CO 121 (139, 157, 177, 195)[215, 233, 253, 271] sts.

RIBBING SETUP ROW (RS): (K1, p1) rep to last st, k1.

Cont in ribbing as est for 12 rows more, ending with a RS row, dec 1 st on last row. 120 (138, 156, 176, 194)[214, 232, 252, 270] sts.

Switch to larger needle.

(WS): P21 (25, 29, 34, 38)[43, 47, 52, 56], pm, p78 (88, 98, 108, 118)[128, 138, 148, 158], pm, purl to end.
DEC ROW (RS): (Knit to 3 sts before m, k2tog, k1, sm, k1, ssk) twice, knit to end. 4 sts dec.

Cont in St st, rep this dec row every 12 rows 4 times more. 100 (118, 136, 156, 174)[194, 212, 232, 250] sts.

Cont in St st for 7 rows, ending with a WS row.

INC ROW (RS): (Knit to 1 st before m, M1R, k1, sm, k1, M1L) twice, knit to end. 4 sts inc.

Rep this inc row every 18th row twice more. 112 (130, 148, 168, 186)[206, 224, 244, 262] sts.

Cont in St st until body meas 16.5 (17, 17.5, 18, 18.5)[19, 19.5, 20, 20.5]" / 42 (43, 44.5, 45.5, 47)[48.5, 49.5, 51, 52] cm or desired length, ending with a WS row.

SHAPE ARMHOLE
(Knit to 2 (4, 5, 7, 8)[10, 11, 13, 14] sts before m, BO 4 (8, 10, 14, 16)[20, 22, 26, 28] underarm sts) twice, knit to end. 17 (19, 22, 25, 28)[31, 34, 37, 40] front sts, 70 (76, 84, 90, 98)[104, 112, 118, 126] back sts.

Cont over left front sts only.

LEFT FRONT
Purl 1 WS row.

DEC ROW (RS): K2, ssk, knit to end. 1 st dec.

Rep this dec row every RS row 1 (1, 4, 7, 9)[11, 13, 15, 17] time(s) more, then every 4th row 1 (2, 1, 0, 0)[0, 0, 0, 0] time(s) more. 14 (15, 16, 17, 18)[19, 20, 21, 22] sts.

Cont in St st until armhole meas 6.5 (7, 7.5, 8, 8.5)[9, 9.5, 10, 10.5]" / 16.5 (18, 19, 20.5, 21.5)[23, 24, 25.5, 26.5) cm, ending with a WS row.

SHAPE SHOULDER
BO 7 (7, 8, 8, 9)[9, 10, 10, 11] sts, knit to end.

Purl 1 WS row.

BO rem 7 (8, 8, 9, 9)[10, 10, 11, 11] sts.

RIGHT FRONT
Return to right front sts, ready to work a WS row.

Purl 1 WS row.

DEC ROW (RS): Knit to last 4 sts, k2tog, k2. 1 st dec.

Rep this dec row every RS row 1 (1, 4, 7, 9)[11, 13, 15, 17] time(s) more, then every 4th row 1 (2, 1, 0, 0)[0, 0, 0, 0] time(s) more. 14 (15, 16, 17, 18)[19, 20, 21, 22] sts.

Cont in St st until armhole matches left front armhole, ending with a RS row.

SHAPE SHOULDER
BO 7 (7, 8, 8, 9)[9, 10, 10, 11] sts, purl to end.

Knit 1 RS row.

BO rem 7 (8, 8, 9, 9)[10, 10, 11, 11] sts.

BACK
Return to back sts, ready to work a WS row.

Purl 1 WS row.

DEC ROW (RS): K2, ssk, knit to last 4 sts, k2tog, k2. 2 sts dec.

Rep this dec row every RS row 1 (1, 4, 7, 9)[11, 13, 15, 17] time(s) more, then every 4th row 1 (2, 1, 0, 0)[0, 0, 0, 0] time(s) more. 64 (68, 72, 74, 78)[80, 84, 86, 90] sts.

Cont in St st until armhole matches left front armhole, ending with a WS row.

SHAPE SHOULDERS
BO 7 (7, 8, 8, 9)[9, 10, 10, 11] sts at beg of next 2 rows, then BO 7 (8, 8, 9, 9)[10, 10, 11, 11] sts at beg of next 2 rows. BO 36 (38, 40, 40, 42)[42, 44, 44, 46] rem back neck sts.

Seam shoulders.

SLEEVES
Beg at center of underarm sts, pick up and knit 2 (4, 5, 7, 8) [10, 11, 13, 14] underarm sts, 26 (28, 30, 31, 33)[35, 37, 38, 40] sts along armhole to shoulder, 26 (28, 30, 31, 33)[35, 37, 38, 40] sts along shoulder to underarm, and 2 (4, 5, 7, 8)[10, 11, 13, 14] underarm sts. 56 (64, 70, 76, 82)[90, 96, 102, 108] sts. Pm and join to work in round.

SHORT ROW 1 (RS): K33 (37, 40, 43, 46)[50, 53, 56, 59], w&t.
SHORT ROW 2 (WS): P10, w&t.
SHORT ROW 3: Knit to wrapped st, knit wrapped st with wrap, w&t.
SHORT ROW 4: Purl to wrapped st, purl wrapped st with wrap, w&t.

Rep Short rows 3 & 4 16 (14, 14, 13, 17)[15, 15, 18, 18] times.

SHORT ROW 5: Knit to 2 sts before wrapped st, k2tog, knit wrapped st with wrap, w&t. 1 st dec.
SHORT ROW 6: Purl to 2 sts before wrapped st, p2tog, purl wrapped st with wrap, w&t. 1 st dec.
SHORT ROW 7: Knit to wrapped st, knit wrapped st with wrap, w&t.
SHORT ROW 8: Purl to wrapped st, purl wrapped st with wrap, w&t.

Rep short rows 5–8 0 (2, 3, 4, 3)[5, 6, 5, 6] times. 54 (58, 62, 66, 74)[78, 82, 90, 94] sts.

NEXT RND: Knit, working wrapped st with its wrap as you come to it.

Knit 7 rnds.

DEC RND: K1, k2tog, knit to last 3 sts, ssk, k1. 2 sts dec.

Cont in St st, rep this dec rnd every 14 (14, 12, 10, 8)[6, 6, 6, 6] rows 6 (6, 2, 2, 6)[14, 10, 6, 2] times more, then every 0 (0, 10, 8, 6)[0, 4, 4, 4] rows 0 (0, 6, 8, 6)[0, 6, 12, 18] times more. 40 (44, 44, 44, 48)[48, 48, 52, 52] sts.

Cont in St st until sleeve meas 14" / 35.5 cm or 4" / 10 cm less than desired length, ending with a WS row.

Switch to smaller needles.

RIBBING SETUP ROW (RS): (K1, p1) rep to end.

Cont in ribbing as est for 4" / 10 cm, ending with a RS row.

Switch to larger needle.

FINISHING
See seamed version for collar instructions.

Weave in all ends. Block to measurements.

Illustrated Guide to Gardening
A FIELD GUIDE TO BIRDS' NESTS
A FIELD GUIDE TO TREES AND SHRUBS
Zoology
MY SIDE OF THE MOUNTAIN
PLUS
HINN
Wirt
GREAT LEADER
PLANTS
Welcome
AN UNCOMMON FREEDOM
FOLLOW YOUR DREAMS

HANCOCK

Hancock *celebrates the comfort of garter stitch, with an extra-wide knitted collar. Fingering weight yarn knitted at a looser gauge contribute to a lightweight garment.*

The pictured sweater was knitted seamless from the top down. If you prefer seamed knits, a second set of instructions is included to knit the cardigan in pieces. This will yield the same result. For more on why you might choose one construction method over the other, *see page 40.*

If you are in-between sizes, I suggest sizing down for an open cardigan like this one. When choosing your size it's always a good idea to check your actual body measurements against all the measurements given in the pattern schematic.

This design is knitted at a loose gauge. To avoid ladders between the joins of double-pointed needles, you may want to use either Magic Loop *or the two circular needle method to knit in the round.* *For more information see page 76.*

FINISHED SIZE

Chest circumference: 31.25 (35.25, 39.25, 43.25, 47.25) [51.25, 55.25, 59.25, 63.25]" / 79.5 (89.5, 100, 110, 120) [130.5, 140.5, 150.5, 161] cm

Shown in 35.25" / 89.5 cm with 2.75" / 7 cm of positive ease.

YARN

7 (8, 10, 11, 12)[14, 15, 17, 18] skeins Quince & Co. *Finch* (100% American wool; 221 yd / 202 m per 50 g skein) in Iceland

OR 1475 (1725, 1975, 2250, 2500)[2825, 3125, 3425, 3750] yd / 1350 (1575, 1800, 2050, 2300)[2575, 2850, 3125, 3450] m of fingering weight yarn

NEEDLES

US 6 / 4 mm:

- 32" /80 cm circular needle
- set of double-pointed needles

Or size needed to obtain gauge.

NOTIONS

Stitch markers, stitch holders or waste yarn, tapestry needle

GAUGE

24 sts and 36 rows = 4" / 10 cm in St st using larger needles.

KNIT SEAMLESS FROM THE TOP DOWN

BEGIN AT TOP

Using circular needle and a long-tail cast on, CO 68 (70, 72, 74, 76)[78, 80, 82, 84] sts.

SETUP ROW (WS): P2, pm, p10, pm, p44 (46, 48, 50, 52)[54, 56, 58, 60], pm, p10, pm, p2.

ROW 1—RAGLAN ONLY INC ROW (RS): (Knit to 1 st before m, M1R, k1, sm, k1 M1L) 4 times, knit to end. 8 sts inc.
ROW 2 (WS): Purl.
ROWS 3–10: Rep last 2 rows 4 times more.
ROW 11—COLLAR AND RAGLAN INC ROW (RS): K1, M1L (knit to 1 st before m, M1R, k1, sm, k1, M1L) 4 times, knit to 1 st from end of row, M1R, k1. 10 sts inc.
ROW 12 (WS): Purl.

Rep rows 1–12 for 3 (3, 4, 5, 5)[6, 7, 7, 8] times more, then rows 1 & 2 for 0 (4, 2, 0, 4)[2, 0, 4, 2] times more. 268 (302, 338, 374, 408)[444, 480, 514, 550] sts: 30 (34, 39, 44, 48)[53, 58, 62, 67] front sts, 58 (66, 74, 82, 90)[98, 106, 114, 122] sleeve sts, 92 (102, 112, 122, 132)[142, 152, 162, 172] back sts.

DIVIDE SLEEVES FROM BODY
(Removing markers as you go, knit to m, place 58 (66, 74, 82, 90)[98, 106, 114, 122] sleeve sts on a stitch holder, CO 2 (4, 6, 8, 10)[12, 14, 16, 18] underarm sts using backward loop cast on) twice, knit to end. 156 (178, 202, 226, 248)[272, 296, 318, 342] sts.

Work 9 (1, 5, 9, 1)[5, 9, 1, 5] row(s) even in St st.

COLLAR ONLY INC ROW (RS): K1, M1L, knit to 1 st before end of row, M1R, k1. 2 sts inc.

Rep this inc row every 12th row 5 times more. 168 (190, 214, 238, 260)[284, 308, 330, 354] sts.

Cont in St st until body meas 8.75 (9, 9, 9.25, 9.25)[9.5, 9.5, 9.5, 9.75]" / 22 (23, 23, 23.5, 23.5)[24, 24, 24, 25] or 2" / 5 cm shorter than desired length.

Work in garter st for 2" / 5 cm.

BO all sts.

SLEEVES

Divide 58 (66, 74, 82, 90)[98, 106, 114, 122] sleeve sts evenly over 3 dpns. With a 4th dpn, pick up and knit 2 (4, 6, 8, 10) [12, 14, 16, 18] sts from underarm edge and pm in the center of the picked up sts to mark the beg of the rnd. Join for working in the rnd, knit to m. 60 (70, 80, 90, 100)[110, 120, 130, 140] sts.

Cont in St st for 8 rnds.

DEC RND: K1, ssk, knit to last 3 sts, k2tog, k1. 2 sts dec.

Rep this dec rnd every 25 (14, 10, 8, 6)[6, 5, 4, 4] rnds 5 (9, 9, 7, 21)[1, 10, 27, 15] time(s) more, then every 0 (0, 9, 7, 0)[5, 4, 3, 3] rnds 0 (0, 4, 10, 0)[24, 19, 6, 22] times more. 48 (50, 52, 54, 56)[58, 60, 62, 64] sts.

Cont in St st until sleeve meas 16" / 40.5 cm or 2" / 5 cm shorter than desired length.

Work in garter st for 2" / 5 cm.

BO all sts.

FINISHING

COLLAR

Using circular needle and beg at the bottom right edge, pick up and knit 3 sts for every 4 rows along right front, then pick up and knit one st for every st around neck edge, then pick up and knit 3 sts for every 4 rows along left front.

Work in garter st for 11" / 28 cm or desired length, ending with a RS row.

BO all sts.

Weave in all ends. Block to measurements.

KNIT IN PIECES AND SEAMED

BACK

Using circular needle and long-tail cast on, CO 96 (108, 120, 132, 144)[156, 168, 180, 192] sts.

Work in garter st for 2" / 5 cm.

Cont in St st until piece meas 10.75 (11, 11, 11.25, 11.25)[11.5, 11.5, 11.5, 11.75]" / 27.5 (28, 28, 28.5, 28.5)[29, 29, 29, 30] cm from CO edge, ending with a WS row.

SHAPE RAGLAN

BO 1 (2, 3, 4, 5)[6, 7, 8, 9] sts at beg of next 2 rows. 94 (104, 114, 124, 134)[144, 154, 164, 174] sts.

DEC ROW (RS): K2, ssk, knit to last 4 sts, k2tog, k2. 2 sts dec.

Rep this dec row every RS row 23 (27, 31, 35, 39)[43, 47, 51, 55] times. 46 (48, 50, 52, 54)[56, 58, 60, 62] sts.

Purl 1 WS row.

BO all sts.

LEFT FRONT

Using larger needle and a long-tail cast on, CO 38 (43, 49, 55, 60)[66, 72, 77, 83] sts.

Work in garter st for 2" / 5 cm.

Cont in St st until piece meas 3 (4.25, 3.75, 3.5, 4.25)[4.25, 3.75, 4.75, 4.5]" / 8 (10.5, 9.5, 9, 11.5)[11, 9.5, 12, 11.5] cm, ending with a WS row.

DEC ROW (RS): Knit to last 3 sts, k2tog, k1. 1 st dec.

Rep this dec row every 12th row 5 times more. 32 (37, 43, 49, 54)[60, 66, 71, 77] sts.

Work 9 (1, 5, 9, 1)[5, 9, 1, 5] row(s) even.

SHAPE RAGLAN

BO 1 (2, 3, 4, 5)[6, 7, 8, 9] st(s), knit to end. 31 (35, 40, 45, 49)[54, 59, 63, 68] sts.

Purl 1 WS row.

SIZES 35.25, 39.25, 47.25, 51.25, 59.25 AND 63.25" / 89.5, 100, 120, 130.5, 150.5 AND 161 CM ONLY

RAGLAN ONLY DEC ROW (RS): K2, ssk, knit to end. 1 st dec.

Rep this dec row every RS row - (3, 1, -, 3)[1, -, 3, 1] time(s) more. - (31, 38, -, 45)[52, -, 59, 66] sts.

Purl 1 WS row.

ALL SIZES

ROW 1—COLLAR AND RAGLAN DEC ROW (RS): K2, ssk, knit last 3 sts, k2tog, k1. 2 sts dec.

ROW 2 (WS): Purl.

ROW 3—RAGLAN ONLY DEC ROW (RS): K2, ssk, knit to end. 1 st dec.

ROWS 4–12: Rep rows 2 & 3 four times more, then work row 2 once more.

Rep rows 1–12 for 3 (3, 4, 5, 5)[6, 7, 7, 8] times more. 3 sts.

BO all sts.

RIGHT FRONT

Using larger needle and a long-tail cast on, CO 38 (43, 49, 55, 60)[66, 72, 77, 83] sts.

Work in garter st for 2" / 5 cm.

Cont in St st until piece meas 3 (4.25, 3.75, 3.5, 4.25)[4.25, 3.75, 4.75, 4.5]" / 8 (10.5, 9.5, 9, 11.5)[11, 9.5, 12, 11.5] cm, ending with a WS row.

DEC ROW (RS): K1, ssk, knit to end. 1 st dec.

Rep this dec row every 12th row 5 times more. 32 (37, 43, 49, 54)[60, 66, 71, 77] sts.

Work 10 (2, 6, 10, 2)[6, 10, 2, 6] rows even.

SHAPE RAGLAN

BO 1 (2, 3, 4, 5)[6, 7, 8, 9] st(s), purl to end. 31 (35, 40, 45, 49)[54, 59, 63, 68] sts.

SIZES 35.25, 39.25, 47.25, 51.25, 59.25 AND 63.25" / 89.5, 100, 120, 130.5, 150.5 AND 161 CM ONLY

RAGLAN ONLY DEC ROW (RS): Knit to last 4 sts, k2tog, k2. 1 st dec.

Rep this dec row every RS row - (3, 1, -, 3)[1, -, 3, 1] time(s) more. - (31, 38, -, 45)[52, -, 59, 66] sts.

Purl 1 WS row.

ALL SIZES

ROW 1—COLLAR AND RAGLAN DEC ROW (RS): K1, ssk, knit to last 4 sts, k2tog, k2. 2 sts dec.

ROW 2 (WS): Purl.

ROW 3—RAGLAN ONLY DEC ROW (RS): Knit to last 4 sts, k2tog, k2. 1 st dec.

ROWS 4–12: Rep rows 2 & 3 four times more, then work row 2 once more.

Rep rows 1–12 for 3 (3, 4, 5, 5)[6, 7, 7, 8] times more. 3 sts.

BO all sts.

SLEEVES

CO 50 (54, 54, 56, 58)[60, 62, 64, 66] sts.

Work in garter st for 2" / 5 cm.

Cont in St st until piece meas 3" / 7.5 cm from CO edge, ending with a WS row.

INC ROW (RS): K2, M1L, knit until 2 sts rem, M1R, k2. 2 sts inc.

Rep this inc row every 26 (14, 10, 8, 6)[6, 6, 4, 4] rows 3 (8, 11, 12, 21)[13, 5, 30, 26] times more, then every 24 (0, 8, 6, 0)[4, 4, 2, 2] rows 2 (0, 2, 5, 0)[12, 24, 3, 11] times more. 62 (72, 82, 92, 102)[112, 122, 132, 142] sts.

Cont in St st until sleeve meas 18" / 45.5 cm, ending with a WS row.

SHAPE RAGLAN

BO 1 (2, 3, 4, 5)[6, 7, 8, 9] sts at beg of next 2 rows. 60 (68, 76, 84, 92)[100, 108, 116, 124] sts.

DEC ROW (RS): K2, ssk, knit to last 4 sts, k2tog, k2. 2 sts dec.

Rep this dec row every RS row 23 (27, 31, 35, 39)[43, 47, 51, 55] times. 12 sts.

Purl 1 WS row.

BO all sts.

FINISHING

Seam raglan lines and underarms. Seam sleeve and side seams.

COLLAR

See seamless version for collar instructions.

Weave in all ends. Block to measurements.

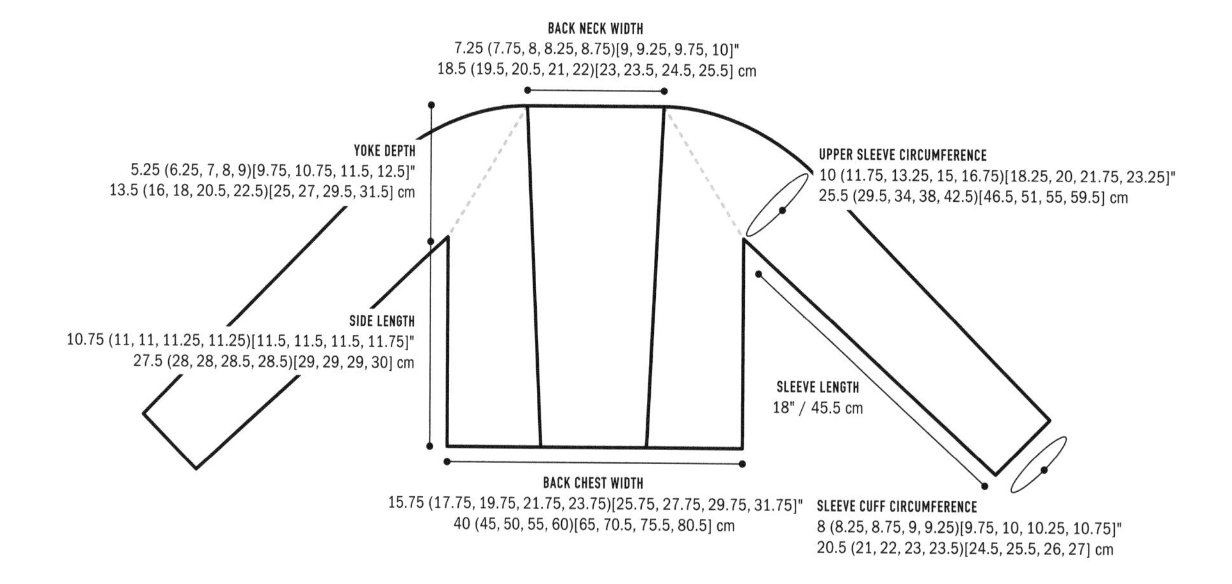

GAUGE

Shut five knitters in a room with the same yarn and needles and it's likely you will end up with five different gauges. This is because we all knit a little differently, achieving different tensions.

Any good knitting book or pattern collection is going to talk about gauge. Most of us understand what it is, and know that it's important. So why are we so tempted to skip this essential step? I'd like to help you resolve to knit nice large gauge swatches, and experience the joy of knitting predictable garments!

When a pattern states a gauge, that is the particular gauge a designer happened to achieve with a particular yarn and needles. If you decide to choose that same yarn and needle size without first testing your results, you can't predict how your garment will come out. Your gauge could be off by a stitch per inch, which over the course of an entire sweater is inches of more or less fabric! On top of that, many of us often choose to substitute a yarn for the one listed in the pattern. In that case, the only way to have any idea of what the results will be is to first knit a gauge swatch.

HOW TO DO IT

First, get on board mentally and emotionally. Remind yourself that by taking the time to knit this gauge swatch, you are ensuring the finished measurements of the piece you are about to spend many hours working on.

Swatch: Next, using the same yarn and needles you will knit your project with, cast on enough stitches for a 6" / 15.5 cm wide swatch. You can work an edge in garter stitch, but you don't have to. Simply knit in the stitch pattern used in the design. In the case of all the pieces in this book that's good ol' Stockinette stitch: knit on the right side, purl on the wrong side. Work in pattern until your swatch measures 6" / 15.5 cm from the cast on row, then bind off.

Block: Once you've completed your swatch you must block it.

If you like quick solutions, you can take a steam iron to your swatch. If you have patience, you can wet block your swatch. To wet block, let your swatch soak in warm, soapy water for five minutes or so. Gently squeeze the water out, and then roll it in a towel to get the remaining water out. Next, spread your swatch out on a blocking board, rug, or towel to dry.

Measure: Now it's time to measure your swatch. Resist the urge to fudge your results by stretching your fabric; let it lay flat and be what it really is. Count your stitches per inch. Is your gauge spot on? Great, now you can use the suggested needle size with confidence. But if it's not, don't be discouraged! If you're getting more stitches per inch, you need to go up a needle size or two. If you're getting fewer stitches per inch you need to go down a needle size or two. And as much as you might be tempted to, you can't just guess and cast on for your garment. Take a deep breath, rip out your first gauge swatch, and knit a new one with your adjusted needle size, to confirm you're going to get your desired gauge

ISSUES

What about row gauge? This is important, too, and hopefully once you achieve your stitch gauge the row gauge will match. But what do we do if it's different?

For example, let's say your target gauge is 6 stitches per inch and 8 rows per inch. You're getting the 6 stitches, but instead of 8 rows you are getting 9 rows per inch. If you're knitting a top down raglan, and the target yoke depth is 7" / 18 cm, your finished yoke will come out 1" / 2.5 cm shorter than intended. You can work with that: you'll just need to be aware of it and add in an extra row or round of knitting for each inch of yoke. In the case of a top down yoke, you can work all the increases as written and then simply knit even until you reach the target yoke depth.

If your gauge is giving you fewer rows per inch than you require, for example if the stated gauge is 8 rows but you're getting 7 rows, knitting as written your yoke will be 1" longer than intended. In this case you'll have to take out a few rows or rounds of knitting. But in my experience, if you're getting stitch gauge you are either going to also get your row gauge or have one row more, not less.

Some knitters feel they have tried and tried and can never get gauge. It has been nothing but an exercise in frustration. To these knitters I say: *Don't give up!* To be a successful sweater knitter, it's essential to nail this exercise. Hopefully this guide can support you as you give it another go.

SOLUTIONS

Here are some practical things you can try. Tension is affected by how you hold your yarn, so you could try tensioning the yarn over or around different fingers. There are different methods of knitting. If you're an English knitter try continental, or vice versa. You can try knitting on a different spot on your needles: perhaps you are knitting too close to the tip. Also, you can try different kinds of needles. Some find it difficult to achieve an even tension using slippery metal needles. You could try wood or even plastic needles and see if that makes a difference. Whatever it takes, find what works for you to make swatching enjoyable!

WHAT IS GAUGE?

It is the number of stitches and rows (or rounds if knit in the round) achieved over 1" / 2.5 cm of knitted fabric.

Gauge is often stated over 4" / 10 cm.

WHAT IS BLOCKING?

Blocking is the step you take to give your yarn a chance to bloom and settle into a smooth even fabric. You can manipulate knit pieces and finished garments to match schematic measurements.

COLLAPSIBLE SHOULDER
6

CHOOSING YOUR SIZE

All of us would love to knit a properly-fitting sweater. Achieving gauge is going to help us do that. We also need to be sure to choose the correct size.

THE SAMPLE SIZE

For reference, the model in this book has an upper torso circumference of 32.5" / 82.5 cm and a full bust circumference of 33.5" / 85 cm.

The ease stated in all patterns is based on her upper torso circumference.

WHAT IS EASE?

Ease is the difference between the measurement of the knitted garment and your body.

Amy Herzog has a lot of good things to say about knitting properly fitting sweaters. When it comes to choosing your size, she says to use your upper torso circumference. This will ensure a good fit in the shoulders, which she says is most important for a flattering sweater. To take this measurement, wrap a tape measure around your chest right under your armpits, above the fullest part of your chest. If you are quite well-endowed, you may want to consult Amy's book or *Craftsy* class, both called *Knit to Flatter*. You can learn how to make a full bust adjustment, along with other adjustments. For most of the cardigans in this collection, open and drapey is the name of the game. You'll be quite safe choosing your size based on your upper torso circumference.

Also keep in mind that chest circumference is not the only measurement provided in a pattern. A schematic for each pattern is provided with many measurements for each size.

EASE

Knits can have positive or negative ease. Negative ease is achieved when the finished circumference of the garment is smaller than the circumference of your body. It's common for a modern knit to call for no ease, meaning it's the same size as your body, or 1–2" of negative ease. It's just as common to find a pattern calling for 1–4" of positive ease, which would mean that the finished circumference of the garment is larger than your body.

If you're unsure of how much ease you like, here's something you can do: Go to your closet and find a knit (it can be a machine knit) that you really like the fit of, something you wear all the time. Measure the chest circumference by laying the knit flat and measuring from armpit to armpit. Take that measurement and multiply it by 2: this is the chest circumference. Now compare this measurement to your body's measurement. Is it smaller, the same, or larger than your chest circumference? You can do the same with other measurements such as the yoke depth, sleeve circumference, and body length, and compare these to the schematic in the pattern. Choose the size closest to the measurements of the much-loved piece from your closet, and you'll no doubt be happy with the finished fit of your sweater.

FIELD
NOTES

ROSEMONT

The oversized fit of Rosemont *makes it an everyday favorite. The compound raglan mimics some of the sleeve cap shaping found with a set-in sleeve construction, which contributes to a comfortable fit. Comfort is also found in using a squishy worsted weight yarn like Quince & Co.* Lark.

The pictured sweater is knitted seamless from the top down. If you prefer seamed knits, a second set of instructions is included to knit the cardigan in pieces. This will yield the same result. For more on why you might choose one construction method over the other, *see page 40.* *In both versions, the bands are picked up and knitted last.*

If you are in-between sizes, I suggest sizing down for an open cardigan like this one. When choosing your size it is always a good idea to check your actual body measurements against all the measurements given in the pattern schematic.

FINISHED MEASUREMENTS

Chest circumference: 34 (37.75, 41.5, 45.25)[49, 52.75, 56.5, 60.25]" / 86 (95.5, 105, 114.5) [124.5, 134, 143.5, 153] cm

Shown in size 34" / 86 cm with 1.5" / 4 cm positive ease.

YARN

9 (10, 11, 12)[13, 14, 16, 17] skeins Quince & Co. *Lark* (100% wool; 134 yd / 123 m per 50 g skein) in Clay

OR 1175 (1300, 1425, 1575) [1725, 1850, 2025, 2175] yd / 1075 (1200, 1300, 1450)[1575, 1700, 1850, 2000] m of worsted weight yarn

NEEDLES

US 9 / 5.5 mm:

- 32" / 80 cm circular needle
- set of double-pointed needles

US 7 / 4.5 mm:

- 32" / 80 cm circular needle
- set of double-pointed needles

Or size needed to obtain gauge.

NOTIONS

Stitch markers, stitch holders or waste yarn, tapestry needle

GAUGE

17 sts and 26 rows = 4" / 10 cm in St st using larger needles

KNIT SEAMLESS FROM THE TOP DOWN

BEGIN AT TOP

Using larger circular needle and a long-tail cast on, CO 84 (86, 88, 90)(92, 94, 96, 98) sts.

SETUP ROW (WS): P3 (front), pm, p20 (sleeve), pm, p38 (40, 42, 44)[46, 48, 50, 52) (back), pm, p20, pm, p3.

ROW 1–RAGLAN AND NECK INC ROW (RS): K1, M1L, (knit to 1 st before m, M1R, k1, sm, k1, M1L) 4 times, knit to 1 st before end of row, M1R, k1. 10 sts inc.
ROW 2 AND ALL WS ROWS: Purl.
ROW 3: Knit.
ROW 5—RAGLAN INC ROW: (Knit to 1 st before m, M1R, k1, sm, k1, M1L) 4 times, knit to end. 8 sts inc.
ROW 7—NECK INC ROW: K1, M1L, knit to 1 st before end of row, M1R, k1. 2 sts inc.
ROW 9—RAGLAN INC ROW: (Knit to 1 st before m, M1R, k1, sm, k1, M1L) 4 times, knit to end. 8 sts inc.
ROW 11: Knit.
ROW 12: Purl.

Work these 12 rows 0 (1, 1, 1)[2, 2, 2, 3] time(s) more, then work row 1 through row 8 (2, 6, 8)[2, 6, 8, 2] once more. 132 (152, 162, 166)[186, 196, 200, 220] sts: 12 (15, 16, 17)[20, 21, 22, 25] front sts, 30 (34, 36, 36)[40, 42, 42, 46] sleeve sts, 48 (54, 58, 60)[66, 70, 72, 78] back sts.

SIZES - (37.75, -, -)[49, -, -, 60.25]" / - (95.5, -, -)[124.5, -, -, 153] CM ONLY

ROW 1—SLEEVE AND BACK ONLY INC ROW: Knit to m, sm, (k1, M1L, knit to last st before m, M1R, k1, sm) 3 times, knit to end. - (158, -, -)[192, -, -, 226] sts: - (15, -, -)[20, -, -, 25] front sts, - (36, -, -)[42, -, -, 48] sleeve sts, - (56, -, -)[68, -, -, 80] back sts.
ROW 2 AND ALL WS ROWS: Purl.
ROW 3–RAGLAN INC ROW: (Knit to 1 st before m, M1R, k1, sm, k1, M1L) 4 times, knit to end. - (166, -, -)[200, -, -, 234] sts: - (16, -, -)[21, -, -, 26] front sts, - (38, -, -)[44, -, -, 50] sleeve sts, - (58, -, -)[70, -, -, 82] back sts.
ROW 5—NECK, SLEEVE AND BACK ONLY INC ROW: K1, M1L, knit to m, sm, (k1, M1L, knit to 1 st before m, M1R, k1, sm) 3 times, knit to 1 st before end of row, M1R, k1. - (174, -, -)[208, -, -, 242] sts: - (17, -, -)[22, -, -, 27] front sts, - (40, -, -)[46, -, -, 52] sleeve sts, - (60, -, -)[72, -, -, 84] back sts.
ROW 6: Purl.

SIZES 41.5 AND 52.75" / 105 AND 134 CM ONLY

ROW 1—NECK, SLEEVE AND BACK ONLY INC ROW: K1, M1L, knit to m, sm, (k1, M1L, knit to 1 st before m, M1R, k1, sm) 3 times, knit to 1 st before end of row, M1R, k1. - (-, 170, -)[-, 204, -, -] sts: - (-, 17, -)[-, 22, -, -] front sts, - (-, 38, -)[-, 44, -, -] sleeve sts, - (-, 60, -)[-, 72, -, -] back sts.
ROW 2: Purl.

ALL SIZES

ROW 1—RAGLAN INC ROW: (Knit to 1 st before m, M1R, k1, sm, k1, M1L) 4 times, knit to end. 8 sts inc.
ROW 2 AND ALL WS ROWS: Purl.

ROW 3—SLEEVE AND BACK ONLY INC ROW: Knit to m, sm, (k1, M1L, knit to last st before m, M1R, k1, sm) 3 times, knit to end. 6 sts inc.
ROW 5—NECK AND RAGLAN INC ROW: K1, M1L, (knit to 1 st before m, M1R, k1, sm, k1, M1L) 4 times, knit to 1 st before end of row, M1R, k1. 10 sts inc.
ROW 7—SLEEVE AND BACK ONLY INC ROW: Knit to m, sm, (k1, M1L, knit to last st before m, M1R, k1, sm) 3 times, knit to end. 6 sts inc.
ROW 9—RAGLAN INC ROW: (Knit to 1 st before m, M1R, k1, sm, k1, M1L) 4 times, knit to end. 8 sts inc.
ROW 11—NECK, SLEEVE AND BACK ONLY INC ROW: K1, M1L, knit to m, sm, (k1, M1L, knit to 1 st before m, M1R, k1, sm) 3 times, knit to 1 st before end of row, M1R, k1. 8 sts inc.
ROW 12: Purl.

Work these 12 rows 0 (0, 0, 1)[0, 1, 1, 1] time(s) more. 178 (220, 216, 258)[254, 296, 292, 334] sts: 17 (22, 22, 27)[27, 32, 32, 37] front sts, 42 (52, 50, 60)[58, 68, 66, 76] sleeve sts, 60 (72, 72, 84)[84, 96, 96, 108] back sts.

SIZES 34, 41.5, 49 AND 56.5" / 86, 105, 124.5 AND 143.5 CM ONLY
ROW 1—RAGLAN INC ROW: (Knit to 1 st before m, M1R, k1, sm, k1, M1L) 4 times, knit to end. 186 (-, 224, -)[262, -, 300, -] sts: 18 (-, 23, -)[28, -, 33, -] front sts, 44 (-, 52, -)[60, -, 68] sleeve sts, 62 (-, 74, -)[86, -, 98] back sts.
ROW 2 AND ALL WS ROWS: Purl.
ROW 3—SLEEVE AND BACK ONLY INC ROW: Knit to m, sm, (k1, M1L, knit to last st before m, M1R, k1, sm) 3 times, knit to end. 192 (-, 230, -)[268, -, 306, -] sts: 18 (-, 23, -)[28, -, 33, -] front sts, 46 (-, 54, -)[62, -, 70, -] sleeve sts, 64 (-, 76, -)[88, -, 100, -] back sts.
ROW 5—NECK AND RAGLAN INC ROW: K1, M1L, (knit to 1 st before m, M1R, k1, sm, k1, M1L) 4 times, knit to 1 st before end of row, M1R, k1. 202 (-, 240, -)[278, -, 316, -] sts: 20 (-, 25, -)[30, -, 35, -] front sts, 48 (-, 56, -)[64, -, 72, -] sleeve sts, 66 (-, 78, -)[90, -, 102, -] back sts.
ROW 6: Purl.

ALL SIZES
DIVIDE SLEEVES FROM BODY
(Removing markers as you go, knit to m, place 48 (52, 56, 60) [64, 68, 72, 76] sleeve sts on a stitch holder, CO 6 (8, 10, 12) [14, 16, 18, 20] underarm sts using a backward loop cast on) twice, knit to end. 118 (132, 148, 162)[178, 192, 208, 222] sts.

Cont in St st for 3 rows.

NECK INC ROW: K1, M1L, knit to 1 st before end of row, M1R, k1. 2 sts inc.

Rep this inc row every 6th row 7 times more. 134 (148, 164, 178)[194, 208, 224, 238] sts.

Cont in St st until body meas 13 (13, 13, 13.25)[13.25, 13.25, 13.5, 13.5]" / 33 (33, 33, 33.5)[33.5, 33.5, 34.5, 34.5] cm from underarm edge, or 3" / 7.5 cm shorter than desired length, ending with a WS row.

Switch to smaller circular needle.

RIBBING SETUP ROW (RS): (K2, p2) rep to last 2 sts, k2.

Cont in ribbing as est for 3" / 7.5 cm.

BO loosely in ribbing.

SLEEVES
Divide 48 (52, 56, 60)[64, 68, 72, 76] held sts evenly over 3 larger dpns. With a 4th dpn, pick up and knit 6 (8, 10, 12)[14, 16, 18, 20] sts along underarm edge and pm in the center of the picked up sts to mark beg of the rnd. Join for working in the rnd, knit to m. 54 (60, 66, 72)[78, 84, 90, 96] sts.

Cont in St st for 5 rnds.

DEC RND: K1, ssk, knit to 3 sts before end of rnd, k2tog, k1. 2 sts dec.

Rep this dec rnd every 11 (8, 7, 6)[5, 5, 4, 4] rnds 8 (11, 4, 13) [16, 4, 22, 13] times more, then every 0 (0, 6, 5)[4, 4, 0, 3] rnds 0 (0, 10, 2)[2, 17, 0, 12] times more. 36 (36, 36, 40)[40, 40, 44, 44] sts.

Cont in St st until sleeve meas 15.5" / 39.5 cm or 3" / 7.5 cm shorter than desired length

Switch to smaller dpns.

RIBBING SETUP RND: (K2, p2) rep to end.

Cont in ribbing as est for 3" / 7.5 cm.

BO loosely in ribbing.

FINISHING
BUTTON BANDS
With smaller circular needle and starting at the lower edge of the right front, pick up and knit 94 (98, 102, 107)[111, 115, 120, 124] sts (approximately two stitches for every three rows) along the right front neck edge, 82 (86, 86, 88)[92, 92, 94, 98] sts along neck edge, then 94 (98, 102, 107)[111, 115, 120, 124] sts along the left front edge. 270 (282, 290, 302) [314, 322, 334, 346] sts.

RIBBING SETUP ROW (WS): (P2, k2) to last 2 sts, p2.

BEGIN SHORT ROWS
SHORT ROW 1 (RS): Work 182 (194, 197, 208)[215, 223, 229, 241] sts in patt, w&t.
SHORT ROW 2 (WS): Work 94 (106, 104, 114)[116, 124, 124, 136] sts in patt, w&t.
SHORT ROW 3: Work in ribbing to wrapped st, pick up wrap and work it together with wrapped st, work 4 sts in patt, w&t.
SHORT ROW 4: Work in ribbing to wrapped st, pick up wrap and work it together with wrapped st, work 4 sts in patt, w&t.

Rep last two rows 9 (10, 10, 11)[11, 12, 12, 13] times.

(RS): Work in patt to end, picking up wrap and working it tog with wrapped st.
(WS): Work in patt to end, picking up wrap and working it tog with wrapped st.

Cont in ribbing for 16 rows more.

BO loosely in ribbing.

KNIT IN PIECES AND SEAMED

BACK

With smaller circular needle, CO 74 (82, 90, 98)[106, 114, 122, 130] sts.

RIBBING SETUP ROW (RS): (K2, p2) rep to last 2 sts, k2.

Cont in ribbing as est for 3" / 7.5 cm.

Switch to larger circular needle.

Work in St st until piece meas 16 (16, 16, 16.25)[16.25, 16.25, 16.5, 16.5]" / 40.5 (40.5, 40.5, 41.5)[41.5, 41.5, 42, 42] cm from CO edge, ending with a WS row.

SHAPE RAGLAN

BO 3 (4, 5, 6)[7, 8, 9, 10] sts at beg of next 2 rows. 68 (74, 80, 86)[92, 98, 104, 110] sts.

DEC ROW (RS): K2, ssk, knit to 4 sts before end of row, k2tog, k2. 2 sts dec

Rep this dec row every RS row 8 (9, 10, 11)[12, 13, 14, 15] times, then every 4th row 5 (6, 7, 8)[9, 10, 11, 12] times. 40 (42, 44, 46)[48, 50, 52, 54] sts.

Purl 1 WS row.

BO all sts.

LEFT FRONT

With smaller circular needle, CO 30 (34, 38, 42)[46, 46, 50, 54] sts.

RIBBING SETUP ROW (RS): (K2, p2) rep to last 2 sts, k2.

Cont in ribbing as est for 3" / 7.5 cm, inc 2 (1, 1, 0)[0 3, 3, 2] st(s) evenly on last row. 32 (35, 39, 42)[46, 49, 53, 56] sts.

Switch to larger circular needle.

Work in St st until piece meas 8.75 (8.75, 8.75, 9)[9, 9, 9.25, 9.25]" / 22.5 (22.5, 22.5, 23)[23, 23, 23.5, 23.5] cm from CO edge, ending with a WS row.

DEC ROW (RS): Knit to last 3 sts, k2tog, k1. 1 st dec.

Rep this dec row every 6 rows 7 times more. 24 (27, 31, 34) [38, 41, 45, 48] sts.

Work 3 rows even.

SHAPE RAGLAN

BO 3 (4, 5, 6)[7, 8, 9, 10] sts at beg of next RS row. 21 (23, 26, 28)[31, 33, 36, 38] sts.

Purl 1 WS row.

SIZES 37.75, 45.25, 52.75 AND 60.25" / 95.5, 114.5, 134 AND 153 CM ONLY

ROW 1—NECK ONLY DEC ROW (RS): Knit to 3 sts before end of row, k2tog, k1. - (22, -, 27)[-, 32, -, 37] sts.
ROW 2 AND ALL WS ROWS: Purl.
ROW 3—RAGLAN ONLY DEC ROW (RS): K2, ssk, knit to end of row. - (21, -, 26)[-, 31, -, 36] sts.
ROW 5: Knit.
ROW 6: Purl.

ALL SIZES

ROW 1—NECK AND RAGLAN DEC ROW (RS): K2, ssk, knit to 3 sts before end of row, k2tog, k1. 2 sts dec.
ROW 2 AND ALL WS ROWS: Purl.
ROW 3: Knit.
ROW 5—RAGLAN ONLY DEC ROW (RS): K2, ssk, knit to end of row. 1 st dec.
ROW 7—NECK ONLY DEC ROW (RS): Knit to 3 sts before end of row, k2tog, k1. 1 st dec.
ROW 9—RAGLAN ONLY DEC ROW (RS): K2, ssk, knit to end of row. 1 st dec.
ROW 11: Knit.
ROW 12: Purl.

Rep these 12 rows 2 (2, 3, 3)[4, 4, 5, 5] times more, then work Rows 1–2 once more. 4 sts.

BO all sts.

RIGHT FRONT

With smaller circular needle, CO 30 (34, 38, 42)[46, 46, 50, 54] sts.

RIBBING SETUP ROW (RS): (K2, p2) rep to last 2 sts, k2.

Cont in ribbing as est for 3" / 7.5 cm, inc 2 (1, 1, 0)[0 3, 3, 2] st(s) evenly on last row. 32 (35, 39, 42)[46, 49, 53, 56] sts.

Switch to larger circular needle.

Work in St st until piece meas 8.75 (8.75, 8.75, 9)[9, 9, 9.25, 9.25]" / 22.5 (22.5, 22.5, 23)[23, 23, 23.5, 23.5] cm from CO edge, ending with a WS row.

DEC ROW (RS): K1, ssk, knit to end of row. 1 st dec.

Rep this dec row every 6 rows 7 times more. 24 (27, 31, 34) [38, 41, 45, 48] sts.

Work 4 rows even.

SHAPE RAGLAN

BO 3 (4, 5, 6)[7, 8, 9, 10] sts, purl to end. 21 (23, 26, 28)[31, 33, 36, 38] sts.

SIZES 37.75, 45.25, 52.75 AND 60.25" / 95.5, 114.5, 134 AND 153 CM ONLY

ROW 1—NECK ONLY DEC ROW (RS): K1, ssk, knit to end of row. - (22, -, 27)[-, 32, -, 37] sts.
ROW 2 AND ALL WS ROWS: Purl.
ROW 3—RAGLAN ONLY DEC ROW (RS): Knit to 4 sts before end of row, k2tog, k2. - (21, -, 26)[-, 31, -, 36] sts.
ROW 5: Knit.
ROW 6: Purl.

ALL SIZES

ROW 1—NECK AND RAGLAN DEC ROW (RS): K1, ssk, knit to 4 sts before end of row, k2tog, k2. 2 sts dec.
ROW 2 AND ALL WS ROWS: Purl.
ROW 3: Knit.

ROW 5—RAGLAN ONLY DEC ROW (RS): Knit to 4 sts before end of row, k2tog, k2. 1 st dec.
ROW 7—NECK ONLY DEC ROW (RS): K1, ssk, knit to end of row. 1 st dec.
ROW 9—RAGLAN ONLY DEC ROW (RS): Knit to 4 sts before end of row, k2tog, k2. 1 st dec.
ROW 11: Knit.
ROW 12: Purl.

Rep these 12 rows 2 (2, 3, 3)[4, 4, 5, 5] times more, then work Rows 1–2 once more. 4 sts.

BO all sts.

SLEEVES

With smaller circular needle, CO 38 (38, 38, 42)[42, 42, 46, 46] sts.

RIBBING SETUP ROW (RS): (K2, p2) rep to last 2 sts, k2.

Cont in ribbing as est for 3" / 7.5 cm, ending with a WS row.

Switch to larger circular needle.

Work 6 rows even in St st, ending with a WS row.

INC ROW (RS): K2, M1L, knit to 2 sts before end of row, M1R, k2. 2 sts inc.

Rep this inc row every 12 (8, 8, 6)[6, 6, 4, 4] rows 4 (11, 2, 14)[8, 2, 22, 19] times more, then every 10 (0, 6, 4)[4, 4, 0, 2] rows 4 (0, 12, 1)[10, 19, 0, 6] time(s) more. 56 (62, 68, 74)[80, 86, 92, 98] sts.

Work in St st until piece meas 18.5" / 47 cm from CO edge, ending with a WS row.

SHAPE RAGLAN

BO 3 (4, 5, 6)[7, 8, 9, 10] sts at beg of next 2 rows. 50 (54, 58, 62)[66, 70, 74, 78] sts.

DEC ROW (RS): K2, ssk, knit to 4 sts before end of row, k2tog, k2. 2 sts dec

Rep this dec row every RS row 8 (9, 10, 11)[12, 13, 14, 15] times, then every 4th row 5 (6, 7, 8)[9, 10, 11, 12] times. 22 sts.

Purl 1 WS row.

BO all sts.

FINISHING

Sew raglan seams. Sew sleeve and side seams.

See seamless version for collar instructions.

Weave in all ends. Block to measurements.

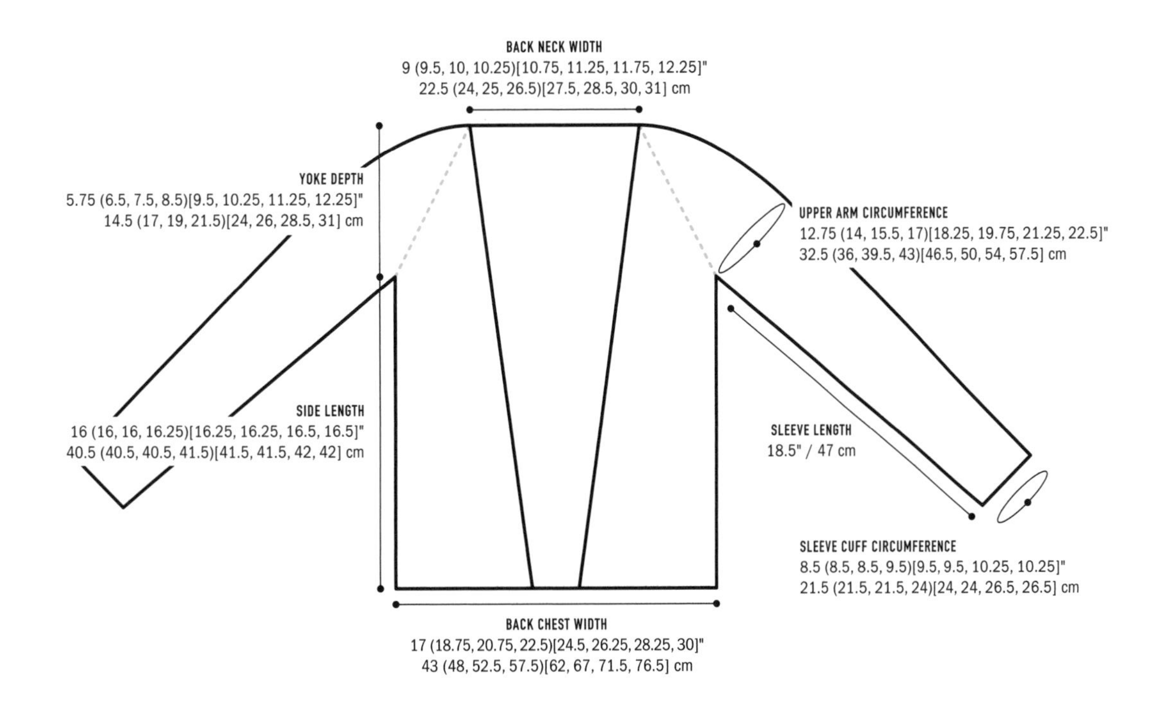

Yashica-A
FIELD
NOTES

SWEATER CONSTRUCTION

Sweaters can be constructed a number of ways. Home & Away *features sweaters with two popular construction methods: set-in sleeve & raglan.*

SET-IN SLEEVE

A set-in sleeve construction (see *Georgetown*, near right and page 12) lends itself well to a more fitted, tailored sweater. It includes a shaped sleeve cap that mimics the shape of the body. Set-in sleeve patterns are most often knit in pieces and seamed, which adds structure to the knit.

RAGLAN

The raglan is a form of a round yoke which doesn't mimic the shape of the body, though yoke shaping can be worked in a variety of ways. There can be a hard diagonal raglan line formed by working increases or decreases at a consistent rate such as every other row or round. A compound raglan such as *Rosemont* (see far right and page 32) tries to mimic the shape of a set in sleeve cap by working increases or decreases at varying rates. Raglans can be knit in three ways so there's room for preference: seamlessly from the bottom up, seamlessly from the top down, and knit in pieces and seamed. The raglans in this book are presented in the latter two ways.

SEAMED VS. SEAMLESS

Sweater knitters usually fall into two camps: those who prefer to knit in pieces and seam, and those who prefer seamless knitting. There are advantages to both methods. Seamed sweaters make for good portable knitting—it's easier to travel with a sleeve in a project bag than an entire seamless sweater. Seams add structure to your sweater. Knit fabric by nature wants to stretch. Seams will help hold everything in its place. When you have a floaty open cardigan such as *Hancock* (page 22), you might not be as concerned about structure. It can still be important, especially if you are working with a fiber that stretches, such as alpaca, cotton or a superwash wool. Good shoulder seams can be important as the entire weight of the garment hangs from these points.

Sweaters can be knit entirely without seams, which for some is a huge plus. Good seaming takes time, and with minimal finishing to work once the seamless sweater is complete, that's time saved. Another advantage of a seamless sweater, particularly a sweater knit from the top down, is that you can try it on and adjust the fit as you go.

SEAMED VERSIONS

All the raglan samples shown in *Home & Away* have been knit seamlessly. However, a second set of instructions has been included to knit the sweater in pieces and then seam. Watch for seamed versions of these knits in the *Home & Away* group on *Ravelry* and the *Home & Away* section of knitbot.com!

PLANTS
Stories of
Legendary
Heroes

Lesley
finished measurements
32 (36, 40, 44)[48, 52, 56, 60]" / 81.5 (91.5, 101.5, 112)[122, 132, 142, 152.5] cm
Suggested ease: positive 0-2" / 0 - 5 cm
yarn
Quince & Co. Osprey (100% wool; 170 yds / 155m per 100g skein) 4 (5, 5, 6)[6, 7, 7, 8] skeins in Petal OR 650 (725, 825, 900)[1000, 1075, 1175, 1275] yards / 600 (675, 750, 825)[900, 975, 1075, 1150] m of aran weight yarn
needles
US 9 / 5.5mm
-16" / 40 cm circular (circ)
-32" / 80 cm circ
-set of double-pointed needles (dpns)
US 10 / 6 mm
-16" / 40 cm circ
-32" / 80 cm circ
-set of dpns
Or size needed to obtain gauge.
notions
Stitch markers (m), tapestry needle
gauge
14 sts and 20 rows = 4" / 10 cm in St st using larger needles.
BEGIN AT TOP
With smaller shorter circ and using the long-tail cast on, CO 86 (88, 90, 92)[94, 96, 98, 100] sts. Join for working in the round, being careful to not twist sts and pm to mark beginning of round.
Ribbing setup round: (K1, p1) repeat to end.
Repeat this round 7 times more.
Switch to larger shorter circ.
Setup round: K24 (25, 26, 27)[28, 29, 30, 31], pm, k19, pm, p24 (25, 26, 27)[28, 29, 30, 31], pm, p19.
SHAPE NECK
Short row 1: K3, w/t
Short row 2: Purl to 4th marker, p3, w/t
Short row 3: Knit to 2 sts past first wrapped st, knitting wrap together with wrapped st as you come to it, w/t
Short row 4: Purl to 2 sts past 2nd wrapped st, purling wrap together with wrapped st as you come to it, w/t
ESTABLISH NECK AND RAGLAN INCREASES
Increase round: (K1, M1L, knit to 1 st before m, M1R, k1) 4 times, slipping markers and knitting wraps together with wrapped sts as you come to them. 8 sts increased.
Repeat this increase round every 4th round twice more, then every other round 0 (0, 2, 2)[4, 4, 6, 6] times more. 110 (112, 130, 132)[150, 152, 170, 172] sts: 30 (31, 36, 37)[42, 43, 48, 49] front/back sts, 25 (25, 29, 29)[33, 33, 37, 37] sleeve sts.
Knit 1 round.
Round 1 - body ONLY increase round: (K1, M1L, knit to 1 st before m, M1R, k1, sm, knit to marker, sm) twice. 4 sts increased.
Round 2: Knit.
Round 3 - sleeve and body increase round: (K1, M1L, knit to 1 st from m, M1R, k1) 4 times, slipping markers as you come to them. 8 sts increased.
Round 4: Knit.
Repeat these 4 rounds 4 (5, 5, 6)[6, 7, 7, 8] times more, then repeat rounds 1 and 2 once more. 174 (188, 206, 220)[238, 252, 270, 284] sts: 52 (57, 62, 67)[72, 77, 82, 87] front/back sts, 35 (37, 41, 43)[49, 53, 55] sleeve sts.
DIVIDE SLEEVES FROM BODY
Removing markers, place 35 (37, 41, 43)[47, 49, 53, 55] sleeve sts on a stitch holder, CO 4 (6, 8, 10)[12, 14, 16, 18] sts for underarm using a backward loop cast on, knit 52 (57, 62, 67)[72, 77, 82, 87] back sts, removing markers place 35 (37, 41, 43)[47, 49, 53, 55] sleeve sts on a holder, CO 4 (6, 8, 10)[12, 14, 16, 18] sts for underarm, knit 52 (57, 62, 67)[72, 77, 82, 87] front sts. 112 (126, 140, 154)[168, 182, 196, 210] sts.
Continue working in the round in St st until body measures 12" / 30.5 cm from underarm edge.
Ribbing setup round: (K1, p1) repeat to end of round.
Continue in ribbing as established for 3" / 7.5 cm.
BO all sts in ribbing.
SLEEVES
Divide 35 (37, 41, 43)[47, 49, 53, 55] sleeve sts evenly over 3 dpns. With a 4th dpn pickup and knit 4 (6, 8, 10)[12, 14, 16, 18] sts from underarm edge and pm in the center of the picked up sts. Join for working in the round, knit to marker. 39 (43, 49, 53)[59, 63, 69, 73] sts.
Continue in St st for 14 (11, 8, 6)[5, 4, 4, 3] rounds.
Decrease round: K1, ssk, knit to last 3 sts, k2tog, k1. 2 sts decreased.
Repeat this decrease round every 15 (12, 9, 7)[6, 5, 5, 4] rounds 3 (3, 5, 9)[9, 13, 5, 15] times more, then every 0 (11, 8, 0)[5, 0, 4, 3] rounds 0 (2, 2, 0)[2, 0, 10, 2] times more. 31 (31, 33, 33)[35, 35, 37, 37] sts.
Continue in St st until sleeve measures 15" / 38 cm or 3" / 7.5 cm shorter than desired length.
ROYAL

UNDERSTANDING A KNITTING PATTERN

If this is your first time knitting a sweater from a pattern, fear not! Here is a breakdown of how to read a knitting pattern, in this case a pattern for a top down seamless raglan.

FINISHED MEASUREMENTS: Here's where you choose your size. Read more about choosing your size on page 30.

YARN: Here's the yarn that was used in the design. You may choose to use the same yarn, or substitute something else using the stated yardage estimate. For tips on yarn substitution, see page 58.

NEEDLES: This is the suggested needle size the designer used to achieve their gauge. But as we learned on page 28, everyone knits differently. When you swatch you may learn that you need to adjust your needle size. Besides the size, the length and type of needles are listed in the order they will be used. For *Lesley* (page 88), the 16" / 40 cm circular will be used at the neck. As you increase for the yoke you'll need to switch to a longer circular needle to accommodate all your stitches. The double-pointed needles are for knitting sleeves in the round. Learn about alternative ways to knit sleeves in the round on page 76.

TOOLS: Here are some other things you'll need to complete your project. Stitch markers are used to divide sections of knitting from each other. You can buy stitch markers from a local yarn shop or craft store. Sometimes I get creative and use things around my house like my daughter's hair bands or safety pins. Stitch holders or waste yarn is used to place live stitches on hold to be worked later. A tapestry needle is a blunt needle with a big eye that will be used to seam the sweater (if necessary) and to weave in loose ends.

GAUGE: Gauge is the most crucial piece of information in the pattern. If you want predictable results, you must achieve the same gauge. Read more about swatching for gauge on page 28.

PATTERN NOTES: Reading the pattern notes will help you understand how the sweater is constructed. It's a good idea to read ahead in the pattern, too, and be sure you get the big-picture view of what you'll be knitting.

Long-tail cast on: A pattern may recommend a cast on. The patterns in this book recommend a long-tail cast on, which is a good default cast on to learn. It's easy to learn and execute, and it provides some elasticity.

Switch to larger / shorter / larger / smaller circ: A pattern will alert you when you need to switch to a different needle size or length.

Setup round: In a setup row or round you will either be placing markers or establishing a stitch pattern that will continue from this point.

Increase round: An increase or decrease round will be labeled as such. Increase rows or rounds in this book recommend two specific methods of increasing, M1L and M1R. Each increase row or round will let you know how many stitches you increased. At the end of the row or round you can double check your stitch count.

Rep this inc rnd every 4th rnd twice more.
110 sts: 30 front sts, 30 back sts, 25 sleeve sts.

Divide Sleeves from Body: Here we'll be placing our sleeve stitches on stitch holders or waste yarn. We'll cast on underarm stitches and then continue working the body, coming back to the sleeves after the body is complete.

SLEEVES: We'll be moving those sleeve stitches from their stitch holders back onto needles and then knitting our sleeves. See page 76 for different methods of knitting sleeves in the round.

Decrease round: Decrease rows or rounds in this book recommend two types of decreases, ssk and k2tog. Each increase row or round will let you know how many stitches you decreased. At the end of the row or round you can double check your stitch count.

Block to measurements: Here's where we truly finish our sweater. To find your target finished measurements check out the schematic. See page 78 for more information on blocking.

SCHEMATIC: More than just finished chest circumference, the schematic contains all sorts of finished measurements. This is helpful when choosing your size and determining if you'd like to make any modifications to the pattern. It also gives you target dimensions for blocking.

CALLIGRAPHY

Calligraphy *cardigan has been a top selling* Knitbot *pattern since 2011, with many beautiful versions completed by knitters around the world. It's truly a classic design for the modern knitter, with a fitted body knit in dk weight yarn, a wide collar, and oversized buttons.*

The pictured sweater is knitted seamless from the top down. If you prefer seamed knits, a second set of instructions is included to knit the cardigan in pieces. This will yield the same result. For more on why you might choose one construction method over the other, see page 40. In both versions, the bands are picked up and knitted last.

If you are in-between sizes, I suggest sizing up for this design. When choosing your size it is always a good idea to check your actual body measurements against all the measurements given in the pattern schematic.

FINISHED MEASUREMENTS
Chest circumference: 35 (38.5, 42.25, 45.5)[49.5, 53, 56.75, 60.25]" / 88.5 (98, 107, 116.5) [125.5, 135, 144, 153.5] cm
Shown in size 35" / 88.5 cm with 2.5" / 6.5 cm of positive ease.

YARN
10 (11, 12, 14)[15, 17, 18, 20] skeins Quince & Co. *Chickadee* (100% wool; 181 yd / 166 m per 50 g skein) in Kumlien's Gull

OR 1575 (1825, 2050, 2300) [2575, 2825, 3100, 3350) yd / 1450 (1675, 1875, 2100)[2350, 2575, 2825, 3050] m of dk weight yarn

NEEDLES
US 6 / 4.0 mm:
- 32" / 80 cm circular needle
- set of double-pointed needles

Or size needed to obtain gauge.

NOTIONS
Stitch markers, stitch holders or waste yarn, split ring markers, tapestry needle, 8 (8, 8, 9)[9, 9, 10, 10] 1.5" / 4 cm buttons, sewing needle and matching thread

GAUGE
22 sts and 28 rows = 4" / 10 cm in St st

KNIT SEAMLESS FROM THE TOP DOWN

BEGIN AT TOP
Using circular needle and a long-tail cast on, CO 94 (102, 106, 110)[118, 122, 126, 130] sts.

RIBBING SETUP ROW (WS): (P2, k2) rep to last 2 sts, p2.

Cont in ribbing until collar meas 7" / 18 cm, ending with a RS row.

SETUP ROW (WS): P14 (15, 16, 17)[18, 19, 20, 21], pm, p10 (12, 12, 12)[14, 14, 14, 14], pm, p46 (48, 50, 52)[54, 56, 58, 60], pm, p10 (12, 12, 12)[14, 14, 14, 14], pm, p14 (15, 16, 17) [18, 19, 20, 21].

SHAPE RAGLAN
INC ROW (RS): (Knit to 1 st before m, M1R, k1, sm, k1, M1L) 4 times, knit to end. 8 sts inc.

Rep this inc row EOR 22 (25, 28, 31)[34, 37, 40, 43] times more. 278 (310, 338, 366) [398, 426, 454, 482] sts: 37 (41, 45, 49)[53, 57, 61, 65] front sts, 56 (64, 70, 76) [84, 90, 96, 102] sleeve sts, 92 (100, 108, 116)[124, 132, 140, 148] back sts.

Purl 1 WS row.

DIVIDE SLEEVES FROM BODY
(Removing markers as you go, knit to m, place 56 (64, 70, 76) [84, 90, 96, 102] sleeve sts on a stitch holder, CO 4 (6, 8, 10) [12, 14, 16, 18] underarm sts using a backward loop cast on and pm in center of cast on sts) twice, knit to end. 174 (194, 214, 234)[254, 274, 294, 314] sts.

Cont in St st for 13 rows, ending with a WS row.

DEC ROW (RS): (Knit to 3 sts before m, k2tog, k1, sm, k1, ssk) twice, knit to end. 4 sts dec.

Rep this dec row every 14 rows twice more. 162 (182, 202, 222)[242, 262, 282, 302] sts.

Cont in St st for 7 rows.

INC ROW (RS): (Knit to 1 st before m, M1R, k1, sm, k1, M1L) twice, knit to end. 4 sts inc.

Rep this inc row every 14 rows 4 times more. 182 (202, 222, 242)[262, 282, 302, 322] sts.

Cont in St st until piece meas 15.5 (16, 16.5, 17)[17.5, 18, 18.5, 19]" / 39.5 (40.5, 42, 43) [44.5, 45.5, 47, 48.5] cm from underarm or 4" / 10 cm shorter than desired length, ending with a WS row.

RIBBING SETUP ROW (RS): (K2, p2) rep to last 2 sts, k2.

Cont in ribbing for 4" / 10 cm.

BO loosely in rib.

SLEEVES
Divide 56 (64, 70, 76)[84, 90, 96, 102] held sleeve sts evenly over 3 dpns. With a 4th dpn pick up and knit 4 (6, 8, 10)[12, 14, 16, 18] sts along underarm edge and pm in the center of the picked up sts to mark the beg of rnd. Join for working in the rnd, knit to m. 60 (70, 78, 86) [96, 104, 112, 120] sts.

Cont in St st for 9 rnds.

DEC RND: K1, ssk, k to last 3 sts, k2tog, k1. 2 sts dec.

Rep this dec rnd every 10 (10, 9, 8)[7, 6, 5, 4] rnds 8 (8, 9, 10) [12, 14, 16, 20] times more. 42 (52, 58, 64)[70, 74, 78, 78] sts.

Cont in St st until sleeve meas 14.5" / 37 cm, or 4" / 10 cm shorter than desired length, dec 2 (0, 2, 0)[2, 2, 2, 2] sts on last rnd. 40 (52, 56, 64)[68, 72, 76, 76] sts.

RIBBING SETUP RND: (K2, p2) rep to end.

Cont in ribbing for 4" / 10 cm.

BO loosely in ribbing.

FINISHING

BUTTONBAND

With circular needle and beg at the left front top edge of collar, pick up and knit 182 (190, 194, 202)[210, 218, 226, 234] sts along left front edge.

RIBBING SETUP ROW (WS): (P2, k2) rep to last 2 sts, p2.

Cont in ribbing until band meas 3" / 7.5 cm.

BO loosely in ribbing.

BUTTONHOLE BAND

With circular needle and beg at the right front bottom edge, pick up and knit 182 (190, 194, 202)[210, 218, 226, 234] sts along right front edge.

RIBBING SET UP ROW (WS): (P2, k2) rep to last 2 sts, p2.

Cont in ribbing for 10 rows, ending with a WS row.

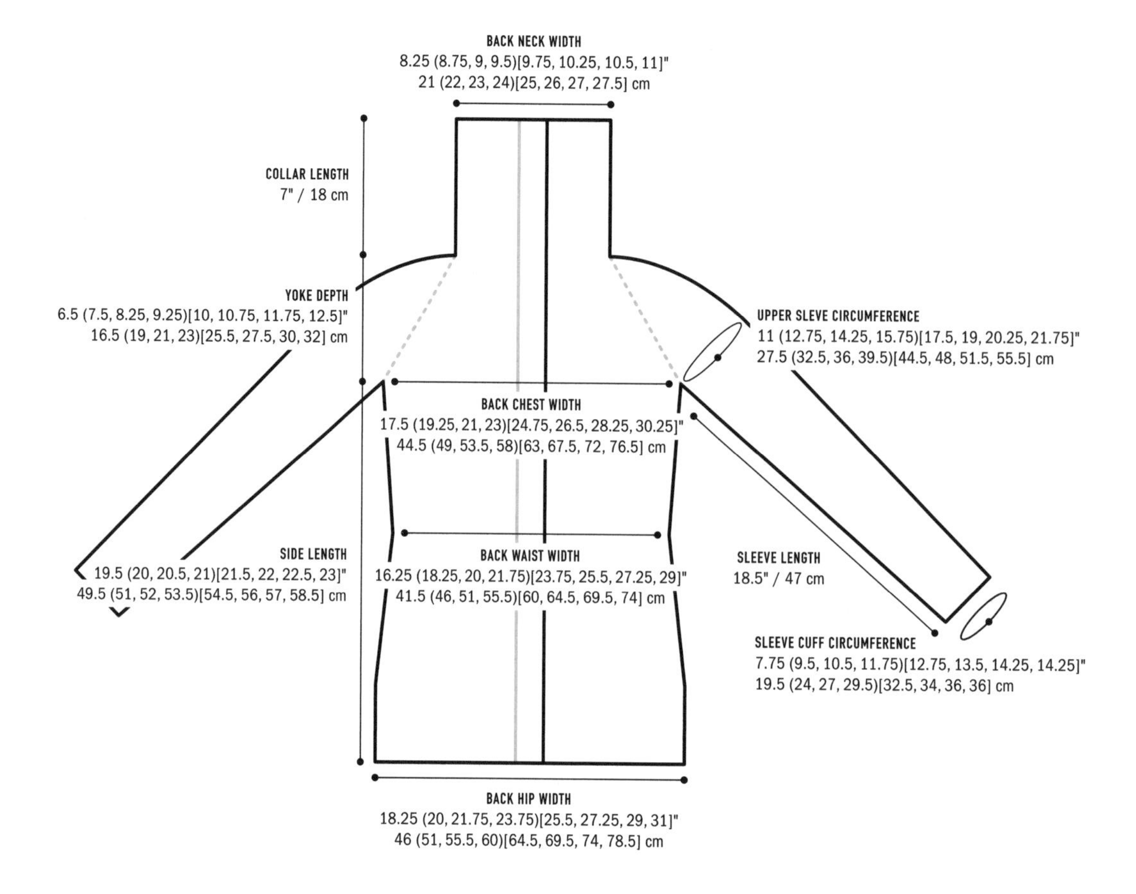

Using locking stitch markers, pm 2" / 5 cm from top edge and 2.5" / 6.5 cm from bottom edge, then place 6 (6, 6, 7)[7, 7, 8, 8] markers spaced evenly between.

BUTTONHOLE ROW (RS): (Work in ribbing to m, sm, work one-row buttonhole [see page 77]) 8 (8, 8, 9)[9, 9, 10, 10] times, work in ribbing to end.

Cont in k2, p2 ribbing until band meas 3" / 7.5 cm.

BO loosely in ribbing.

Place buttons to correspond with buttonholes. Stitch in place.

Weave in all ends. Block to measurements.

KNIT IN PIECES AND SEAMED

BACK

Using circular needle and a long-tail cast on, CO 102 (112, 122, 132)[142, 152, 162, 172] sts.

RIBBING SETUP ROW (WS): P2 (1, 1, 3)[2, 1, 1, 3], k0 (0, 1, 0)[0, 0, 1, 0], p0 (0, 2, 0)[0, 0, 2, 0], (k2, p2) to last 0 (3, 2, 1) [0, 3, 2 1] st(s), k0 (2, 1, 0)[0, 2, 1, 0), p0 (1, 1, 1)[0, 1, 1, 1].

Cont in ribbing for 4" / 10 cm.

Cont in St st until piece meas 4.5 (5, 5.5, 6)[6.5, 7, 7.5, 8]" / 11.5 (12.5, 14, 15)[16.5, 18, 19, 20.5] cm, ending with a WS row.

DEC ROW (RS): K2, ssk, knit to last 4 sts, k2tog, k2. 2 sts dec.

Rep this dec row every 14 rows 4 times more. 92 (102, 112, 122)[132, 142, 152, 162] sts.

Cont in St st for 7 rows.

INC ROW (RS): K2, M1L, knit to last 2 sts, M1R, k2. 2 sts inc.

Rep this inc row every 14 rows twice more. 98 (108, 118, 128) [138, 148, 158, 168] sts.

Cont in St st until piece meas 19.5 (20, 20.5, 21)[21.5, 22, 22.5, 23]" / 49.5 (51, 52, 53.5)[54.5, 56, 57, 58.5] cm, ending with a WS row.

SHAPE RAGLAN

BO 2 (3, 4, 5)[6, 7, 8, 9] sts at beg of next 2 rows. 94 (102, 110, 118)[126, 134, 142, 150] sts.

DEC ROW (RS): K2, ssk, knit to last 4 sts, k2tog, k2. 2 sts dec.

Rep this dec row every RS row 22 (25, 28, 31)[34, 37, 40, 43] times more. 48 (50, 52, 54) [56, 58, 60, 62] sts.

Purl 1 WS row.

BO all sts.

LEFT FRONT
Using circular needle and a long-tail cast on, CO 42 (47, 52, 57)[62, 67, 72, 77] sts.

RIBBING SETUP ROW (WS): P2 (3, 1, 1)[2, 3, 1, 1], k0 (0, 1, 0)[0, 0, 1, 0], p0 (0, 2, 0)[0, 0, 2, 0], (k2, p2) rep to end.

Cont in ribbing for 4" / 10 cm.

Cont in St st until piece meas 4.5 (5, 5.5, 6)[6.5, 7, 7.5, 8]" / 11.5 (12.5, 14, 15)[16.5, 18, 19, 20.5] cm, ending with a WS row.

DEC ROW (RS): K2, ssk, knit to end. 1 st dec.

Rep this dec row every 14 rows 4 times more. 37 (42, 47, 52) [57, 62, 67, 72] sts.

Cont in St st for 7 rows.

INC ROW (RS): K2, M1L, knit to end. 1 st inc.

Rep this inc row every 14 rows twice more. 40 (45, 50, 55)[60, 65, 70, 75] sts.

Cont in St st until piece meas 19.5 (20, 20.5, 21)[21.5, 22, 22.5, 23]" / 49.5 (51, 52, 53.5) [54.5, 56, 57, 58.5] cm, ending with a WS row.

SHAPE RAGLAN
BO 2 (3, 4, 5)[6, 7, 8, 9] sts, knit to end. 38 (42, 46, 50)[54, 58, 62, 66] sts.

Purl 1 row.

DEC ROW (RS): K2, ssk, knit to end. 1 st dec.

Rep this dec row every RS row 22 (25, 28, 31)[34, 37, 40, 43] times more. 15 (16, 17, 18) [19, 20, 21, 22] sts.

Purl 1 WS row.

BO all sts.

RIGHT FRONT
Using circular needle and a long-tail cast on, CO 42 (47, 52, 57)[62, 67, 72, 77] sts.

RIBBING SETUP ROW (WS): (P2, k2) rep to last 2 (3, 4, 1)[2, 3, 4, 1] st(s), p2 (3, 2, 1)[2, 3, 2, 1], k0 (0, 1, 0)[0, 0, 1, 0], p0 (0, 1, 0)[0, 0, 1, 0].

Cont in ribbing for 4" / 10 cm.

Cont in St st until piece meas 4.5 (5, 5.5, 6)[6.5, 7, 7.5, 8]" / 11.5 (12.5, 14, 15)[16.5, 18, 19, 20.5] cm, ending with a WS row.

DEC ROW (RS): Knit to last 4 sts, k2tog, k2. 1 st dec.

Rep this dec row every 14 rows 4 times more. 37 (42, 47, 52) [57, 62, 67, 72] sts.

Cont in St st for 7 rows.

INC ROW (RS): Knit to last 2 sts, M1R, k2. 1 st inc.

Rep this inc row every 14 rows twice more. 40 (45, 50, 55)[60, 65, 70, 75] sts.

Cont in St st until piece meas 19.5 (20, 20.5, 21)[21.5, 22, 22.5, 23]" / 49.5 (51, 52, 53.5) [54.5, 56, 57, 58.5] cm, ending with a RS row.

SHAPE RAGLAN
BO 2 (3, 4, 5)[6, 7, 8, 9] sts, purl to end. 38 (42, 46, 50)[54, 58, 62, 66] sts.

DEC ROW (RS): Knit to last 4 sts, k2tog, k2. 1 st dec.

Rep this dec row every RS row 22 (25, 28, 31)[34, 37, 40, 43] times more. 15 (16, 17, 18) [19, 20, 21, 22] sts.

Purl 1 WS row.

BO all sts.

SLEEVES
Using circular needle and a long-tail cast on, CO 44 (52, 60, 64)[72, 76, 80, 80] sts.

RIBBING SETUP ROW (WS): (P2, k2) rep to end.

Cont in ribbing for 4" / 10 cm, ending with a WS row.

Cont in St st for 6 rows.

INC ROW (RS): K1, M1L, knit to last 2 sts, M1R, k2. 2 sts inc.

Rep this inc row every 12 (10, 10, 8)[8, 8, 6, 6] rows 3 (7, 7, 10)[7, 1, 11, 3] time(s) more, then every 10 (8, 8, 6)[6, 6, 4, 4] rows 5 (2, 2, 1)[5, 13, 5, 17] time(s) more. 62 (72, 80, 88)[98, 106, 114, 122] sts.

Cont in St st until piece meas 18.5" / 47 cm, ending with a WS row.

SHAPE RAGLAN
BO 2 (3, 4, 5)[6, 7, 8, 9] sts at beg of next 2 rows. 58 (66, 72, 78)[86, 92, 98, 104] sts.

DEC ROW (RS): K2, ssk, knit to last 4 sts, k2tog, k2. 2 st dec.

Rep this dec row every RS row 22 (25, 28, 31)[34, 37, 40, 43] times more. 12 (14, 14, 14) [16, 16, 16, 16] sts.

Purl 1 WS row.

BO all sts.

FINISHING
Seam raglan and underarms. Seam sleeve and side seams.

COLLAR
Using circular needle, pick up and knit 94 (102, 106, 110) [118, 122, 126, 130] sts along neck edge.

RIBBING SETUP ROW (WS): (K2, p2) rep to end, k2.

Cont in ribbing until collar meas 7" / 18 cm.

BO all sts.

BUTTON AND BUTTONHOLE BANDS
See seamless version for band instructions.

Weave in all ends. Block to measurements.

SIMPLE HAT

I originally designed this simple hat pattern as part of a knit-a-long demonstrating how to knit a properly fitting hat.

The key, as with all knitting, is to be sure you first knit a gauge swatch. Once you're sure you are getting gauge, choose a circumference that is 0–2" / 0–5 cm smaller than your actual head circumference. Negative ease will ensure a properly fitting hat!

This pattern includes instructions for hats in five sizes at three different gauges!

TO FIT

Baby 16" (Toddler 18", Child 20", Adult 22", XL Adult 24")

Shown in version C with 1.5" / 4 cm of negative ease; suggested negative ease of 0–2" / 0–5 cm

VERSION A: BULKY WEIGHT

FINISHED CIRCUMFERENCE: 15 (17, 19, 21, 23)" / 38 (43, 48, 53, 58) cm

FINISHED HEIGHT: 6 (6.75, 7.75, 8.75, 9.75)" /15.25 (17, 19.5, 22.25, 24.75) cm

YARN: 1 skein Quince & Co. *Osprey* (100% American wool; 170 yd / 155 m per 100 g skein) OR 45 (56, 70, 88, 110) yd / 41 (51, 64, 80, 100) m of bulky weight yarn

NEEDLES: US 9 / 5.5 mm 16" / 40 cm circular; US 10 / 6.0 mm 16" / 40 cm circular and set of double-pointed needles

NOTIONS: Stitch markers, tapestry needle

GAUGE: 14 sts and 20 rows = 4" / 10 cm in St st

VERSION B: WORSTED WEIGHT

FINISHED CIRCUMFERENCE: 14.5 (16.75, 19.25, 20.75, 22.5)" / 37 (42.5, 49, 52.75, 57.25) cm

FINISHED HEIGHT: 5.5 (6.25, 7.25, 8.5, 9.75)" / 14 (15.75, 18.25, 21.5, 24.75) cm

YARN: 1 (1, 1, 2, 2) skein(s) Quince & Co. *Lark* (100% American wool; 134 yd / 123 m per 50 g skein) OR 75 (95, 115, 140, 170) yd / 69 (87, 105, 125, 155) of worsted weight yarn

NEEDLES: US 5 / 3.75 mm 16" / 40 cm circular; US 7 / 4.5 mm 16" / 40 cm circular and set of double-pointed needles

NOTIONS: Stitch markers, tapestry needle

GAUGE: 20 sts and 28 rows = 4" / 10 cm in St st

VERSION C: DK WEIGHT

FINISHED CIRCUMFERENCE: 15 (16.25, 18.75, 21, 22.75)" / 38 (41.25, 47.75, 53, 57.75) cm

FINISHED HEIGHT: 5.75 (7, 7.25, 8.5, 9.5)" / 14.5 (17.75, 18.25, 21.5, 24) cm

YARN: 1 (1, 1, 2, 2) skein(s) Quince & Co. *Chickadee* (100% American wool; 170 yd / 155 m per 100 g skein) in Kumlien's Gull OR 92 (116, 144, 180, 215) / 84 (106, 132, 165, 197) m of dk weight yarn

NEEDLES: US 3 / 3.25 mm 16" / 40 cm circular; US 5 / 3.75 mm 16" / 40 cm circular and set of double-pointed needles

NOTIONS: Stitch markers, tapestry needle

GAUGE: 24 sts and 32 rows = 4" / 10 cm in St st

VERSION A: BULKY WEIGHT

With smaller circular needle and using a long-tail cast on, CO 48 (56, 64, 72, 80) sts.

Pm and join for working in the rnd, being careful not to twist sts.

SETUP RND: (K1, p1) rep to end of rnd.

Cont in k1, p1 ribbing until band meas 1.5 (2, 2.5, 3, 3)" / 3.75 (5, 6.25, 7.75, 7.75) cm from CO edge.

Switch to larger circular needle.

Cont in St st until hat meas 3.25 (4, 5, 6, 7)" / 5.75 (10.25, 12.75, 15.25, 17.75) cm from CO edge.

NOTE: If you'd like a slouchier cap, knit 1–2" / 2.5–5 cm more in St st then proceed as instructed. You will also need extra yarn if you do so.

BEGIN CROWN SHAPING

SETUP RND: (Knit 8, pm) rep to end of rnd.
DEC RND: (Knit to 2 sts before m, k2tog, sm) rep to end of rnd—6 (7, 8, 9, 10) sts dec.

Rep this dec rnd EOR until 6 (7, 8, 9, 10) sts rem. Switch to dpns when necessary.

NEXT RND: K2tog 3 (3, 4, 4, 5) times, k0 (1, 0, 1, 0). 3 (4, 4, 5, 5) sts.

FINISHING

Cut yarn leaving a tail. Thread tail of yarn onto a tapestry needle and using a duplicate stitch, weave the end into the WS of the hat. Gently block.

VERSION B: WORSTED WEIGHT

With smaller circular needle and using a long-tail cast on, CO 72 (84, 96, 104, 112) sts.

Pm and join for working in the rnd, being careful not to twist sts.

SETUP RND: (K1, p1) rep to end of rnd.

Cont in k1, p1 ribbing until band meas 1.5 (2, 2.5, 3, 3)" / 3.75 (5, 6.25, 7.75, 7.75) cm from CO edge.

Switch to larger circular needle.

Cont in St st until hat meas 2.5 (3.25, 4.25, 5.25, 6)" / 6.25 (8.25, 10.75, 13.25, 15.25) cm from CO edge.

NOTE: If you'd like a slouchier cap, knit 1–2" / 2.5–5 cm more in St st then proceed as instructed. You will also need extra yarn if you do so.

BEGIN CROWN SHAPING

SETUP RND: [K12 (12, 12, 13, 14), pm] rep to end of rnd.
DEC RND: (Knit to 2 sts before m, k2tog, sm) rep to end of rnd—6 (7, 8, 8, 8) sts dec.

Rep this dec rnd EOR until 6 (7, 8, 8, 8) sts rem. Switch to dpns when necessary.

NEXT RND: K2tog 3 (3, 4, 4, 4) times, k0 (1, 0, 0, 0). 3 (4, 4, 4, 4) sts.

FINISHING

Cut yarn leaving a tail. Thread tail of yarn onto a tapestry needle and using a duplicate stitch, weave the end into the WS of the hat. Gently block.

VERSION C: DK WEIGHT

With smaller circular needle and using a long-tail cast on, CO 90 (98, 112, 126, 136) sts.

Pm and join for working in the rnd, being careful not to twist sts.

SETUP RND: (K1, p1) rep to end of rnd.

Cont in k1, p1 ribbing until band meas 1.5 (2, 2.5, 3, 3)" / 3.75 (5, 6.25, 7.75, 7.75) cm from CO edge.

Switch to larger circular needle.

Cont in St st until hat meas 3.5 (3.75, 4, 4.25, 5.5)" / 9 (9.5, 10.25, 10.75, 14) cm from CO edge.

NOTE: If you'd like a slouchier cap, knit 1–2" / 2.5–5 cm more in St st then proceed as instructed. You will also need extra yarn if you do so.

BEGIN CROWN SHAPING

SETUP RND: [K10 (14, 14, 18, 17), pm] rep to end of rnd.

DEC RND: (Knit to 2 sts before m, k2tog, sm) rep to end of rnd—9 (7, 8, 7, 8) sts dec.

Rep this dec rnd EOR until 9 (7, 8, 7, 8) sts rem. Switch to dpns when necessary.

NEXT RND: K2tog 4 (3, 4, 3, 4) times, k1 (1, 0, 1, 0). 5, (4, 4, 4, 4) sts.

FINISHING

Cut yarn leaving a tail. Thread tail of yarn onto a tapestry needle and using a duplicate stitch, weave the end into the WS of the hat. Gently block.

© Matt Barter

For *Home & Away* I worked exclusively with yarn from a company near and dear to my heart: Quince & Co. What makes this company so special? First of all, I love the people of Quince. Also, their yarns! Spun from fibers sourced with care here in the United States, and featuring the most exquisite color palette you'll find on a yarn store shelf, this is my yarn—it makes up 90% of my stash.

For this collection I worked primarily with neutrals, with the exception of the warm terra cotta color called clay. I also used a few gray heathers. But that isn't to say that you can't choose to knit yourself a cardigan or pullover in a bold, rich color! Personally I like the versatility of sweaters in neutrals paired with fun, colorful accessories. Also, when I'm building a wardrobe I like all the colors to work together, in addition to looking beautiful on their own.

QUINCE & CO. FOUNDER PAM ALLEN TALKS ABOUT HER COMPANY AND YARN

Hannah Fettig: Pam! You worked in the industry for many years before starting your own yarn company. What led to your starting Quince & Co.?

Pam Allen: I learned that there was an old spinning mill down the road in Biddeford, Maine, that had lapsed into making bridle cord for horses (still its bread and butter product). Recently the owner had begun to make knitting yarn. I couldn't resist—I was over there introducing myself in a heartbeat. One thing led to another and I decided to work with the mill to make a line of U.S.-sourced wool yarn.

Hannah: It isn't easy to make yarn here in the U.S. What are some of the challenges, and what positive things do you see happening on this front?

Pam: It's difficult to make yarn in the U.S. for a variety of reasons. Most of the facilities have closed and the few that remain struggle with equipment that often isn't set up to work with wool fiber. After World War II, when synthetics were the rage, the mills that managed to stay in business often switched their machinery for the new fibers. Sadly, when the demand for wool yarn came around again, the mills weren't always equipped as well as they might have been.

The mill we use primarily is set up for wool spinning, but the equipment is from the early part of the 20th century. Impossible to find parts.

Ancillary businesses, wool processing, combing and carding facilities, dye houses, etc., are almost non-existent. Yes, a few places remain, but the services they offer are limited. And now that demand is stepping up (a good thing!), they often are too busy to turn things around quickly. So timing and supply are always a challenge.

It's also expensive to make yarn in this country. We pay better wages, as we should, than companies abroad do and we have careful environmental and safety standards to adhere to. A good thing. But this makes it harder to compete with less expensive yarn from overseas.

What I love, though, about making yarn here, in spite of the problems, is that I meet the most wonderful people. I love the spinners who've managed against the odds to find a way to stay in business. They're my heroes. I want to give them all the work I can. I love that there are still sheep ranches in this country and that, however small our business is, we're a small part of the demand for their fiber. The more sheep, the fewer parking lots.

Hannah: You have a wonderful eye for color. How did you come up with the original Quince color palette? And where is the palette headed?

Pam: Choosing colors is one of the best parts of my job. Carrie Hoge—who worked with me at the beginning—and I chose the colors. We wanted a lot of neutrals and soft colors—the colors we like to wear. Then we added deep colors, a good teal, bark brown, and purple, then airy light blues and pinks, and a few brights, like Nasturtium, a bold red-orange. We started with 37 colors, we now have over 50. I'd love to keep adding until we have a solid 80 or so. There's always another color that I think we could use. Just today, someone in the office was saying we need a good "saffron" yellow. A spicy palette may be up next.

Hannah: Favorites can be ever changing—what is your current favorite Quince & Co. yarn?

Pam: Owl, *our wool/alpaca blend. It's so buoyant and soft. I adore it.*

Hannah: If someone has never tried a Quince & Co yarn before, what can they expect?

Pam: A quality yarn, well balanced, as soft as it can be and still be durable. In a lot of colors.

Pam Allen is the founder of Quince & Co. (www.quinceandco.com)

WHEN SUBSTITUTING YARN, WHAT SHOULD YOU KEEP IN MIND?

Understandably, we can't always use the suggested yarn in a pattern. Availability, personal preference, and budget may dictate otherwise. If you will be substituting yarn, consider the fiber content of the yarn used in the design and think about what it brings to the table. Is it providing stitch definition or drape? Is it light and airy, or dense? Loose or tightly twisted? The designs in this book are simple and leave a lot of room for improvisation. You could knit at a loose gauge by choosing a finer yarn and knitting it on a larger needle and still achieve the stated gauge. You can knit from your stash or shop for different yarns that have properties you especially like, such as the halo of angora or the vibrancy of an indy hand dye. After you've knit and blocked your gauge swatch, hold it up and watch how the fabric behaves. Envision an entire sweater knit in this fabric: will you be happy with it?

KNITTING FROM YOUR "STASH"

Most crafters have a stash. Various materials may have been purchased both purposefully and spontaneously. It's common to have trouble actually knitting from your stash. Here are some things you can do:

BUY MORE PURPOSEFULLY.

If you're shopping and stumble across something you love, take a deep breath. Resist the urge to buy a ton of it to reflect how much you love it. Once the heart palpitations and sweating have subsided, try to think about what you would want to use this material for. You might not yet have something specific in mind—or maybe you have too many things! Can you narrow it down? Do you want to make something for a child or for an adult? What would this material be best suited for?

DEALING WITH STASH GUILT.

You don't have to force yourself to work from your stash if you really aren't finding the right fit for a particular project. You're less likely to enjoy working on the project, and you might not like the finished result. A better way to approach your stash may be to start with the material, fall in love with it again, and then chose a project that suits it. On the other hand, sometimes we save materials for too long because we love them so much. We want to be sure they match up with just the right project. There have been cases where I held on to something for years. And then what happened? I'm not in love with it anymore. If you really love a yarn in your stash, don't stress, just *use it*. Power through the doubts and create *something* with the material. In most cases you'll be very happy with the finished project.

GET ORGANIZED.

Take a few hours to organize your materials in a pleasing manner. I'm not a big fan of storing things in ziplock bags inside plastic bins. I like to have everything out, sorted by color or coordinates, so it can inspire me on a day to day basis. I shuffle everything around from time to time to give me a fresh perspective.

If you're interested in building a more useful stash, you can check out my stash-buying guide *StashBot*, available both in print and as an interactive app, at www.knitbot.com/stashbot

WHAT IS A STASH?

It's your personal collection of yarn or other knit-related materials you've collected and "stashed" over time.

BOOTHBAY

Boothbay *is a cocoon of a cardigan, cradling you with its cozy garter stitch collar. Knitted in worsted weight yarn, the long body and wide open front make it perfect for everyday wear.*

The pictured sweater is knitted seamless from the top down. If you prefer seamed knits, a second set of instructions is included to knit the cardigan in pieces. This will yield the same result. For more on why you might choose one construction method over the other, see page 40. In both versions, the collar is picked up and knitted last.

If you are in-between sizes, I suggest sizing down for an open cardigan like this one. When choosing your size it is always a good idea to check your actual body measurements against all the measurements given in the pattern schematic.

FINISHED MEASUREMENTS
Chest circumference: 31.25 (35.25, 39.25, 43.25, 47.25) [51.25, 55.25, 59.25, 63.25]" / 79 (89.5, 99.5, 109.5, 120) [130, 140, 150.5, 160.5] cm
Shown in size 35.25" / 89.5 cm with 2.75" / 7 cm positive ease.

YARN
11 (12, 13, 14, 16)[17, 18, 20, 21] skeins Quince & Co. *Lark* (100% American wool; 134 yd / 123 m per 50 g skein) in Bark

OR 1400 (1525, 1725, 1875, 2050)[2225, 2400, 2600, 2800] yd / 1275 (1400, 1575, 1700, 1875)[2050, 2200, 2375, 2550] m of worsted weight yarn

NEEDLES
US 7 / 4.5 mm:
- 32" / 80 cm circular needle
- set of double-pointed needles

Or size needed to obtain gauge.

NOTIONS
Stitch markers, stitch holders or waste yarn, tapestry needle

GAUGE
20 sts and 28 rows = 4" / 10 cm in St st

KNIT SEAMLESS FROM THE TOP DOWN

BEGIN AT TOP
Using circular needle and a long-tail cast on, CO 72 (74, 76, 78, 80)[82, 84, 86, 88] sts.

SETUP ROW (WS): P2, pm, p14, pm, p40 (42, 44, 46, 48)[50, 52, 54, 56], pm, p14, pm, p2.

ESTABLISH RAGLAN INCREASES
INC ROW (RS): Knit to 1 st before m, M1R, k1, sm, (k1, M1L, knit to 1 st before m, M1R, k1, sm) 3 times, k1, M1L, knit to end. 8 sts inc.

Cont in St st, rep this inc row every RS row 10 (13, 17, 20, 24)[27, 31, 34, 38] times more. 160 (186, 220, 246, 280)[306, 340, 366, 400] sts: 13 (16, 20, 23, 27)[30, 34, 37, 41] front sts, 36 (42, 50, 56, 64)[70, 78, 84, 92] sleeve sts, 62 (70, 80, 88, 98)[106, 116, 124, 134] back sts.

Purl 1 WS row.

ROW 1—FRONTS ONLY INC ROW (RS): Knit to 1 st before m, M1R, (knit to m, sm) 3 times, k1, M1L, knit to end. 2 sts inc.
ROW 2 (WS): Purl to end.
ROW 3—RAGLAN INC ROW (RS): Knit to 1 st before m, M1R, k1, sm, (k1, M1L, knit to 1 st before m, M1R, k1, sm) 3 times, k1, M1L, knit to end. 8 sts inc.
ROW 4 (WS): Purl to end.

Rep rows 1–4 for 5 (5, 4, 4, 3)[3, 2, 2, 1] time(s) more. 220 (246, 270, 296, 320)[346, 370, 396, 420] sts: 25 (28, 30, 33, 35)[38, 40, 43, 45] front sts, 48 (54, 60, 66, 72)[78, 84, 90, 96] sleeve sts, 74 (82, 90, 98, 106)[114, 122, 130, 138] back sts.

DIVIDE SLEEVES FROM BODY
(Removing markers as you go, knit to m, place 48 (54, 60, 66, 72)[78, 84, 90, 96] sleeve sts onto a stitch holder, using a backward loop cast on CO 4 (6, 8, 10, 12)[14, 16, 18, 20] underarm sts) twice, knit to end. 132 (150, 166, 184, 200)[218, 234, 252, 268] sts.

Cont in St st for 7 rows.

DEC ROW (RS): K1, ssk, knit to last 3 sts, k2tog, k1. 2 sts dec.

Rep this dec row at center edge every 10 (8, 10, 8, 10)[8, 8, 8, 8] rows 3 (8, 2, 6, 1)[4, 5, 2, 3] time(s) more, every 8 (0, 8, 6, 8)[6, 0, 6, 6] rows 5 (0, 5, 1, 5)[2, 0, 3, 1] time(s), then every RS row 18 (22, 26, 30, 34)[38, 42, 46, 50] times. 78 (88, 98, 108, 118)[128, 138, 148, 158] sts.

Purl 1 WS row.

BO all sts.

SLEEVES
Divide 48 (54, 60, 66, 72)[78, 84, 90, 96] held sleeve sts over 3 dpns. With a 4th dpn, pick up and knit 4 (6, 8, 10, 12)[14, 16, 18, 20] sts from the underarm edge, pm in the center of the picked up sts to mark beg of the rnd. Join for working in the rnd, knit to m. 52 (60, 68, 76, 84)[92, 100, 108, 116] sts.

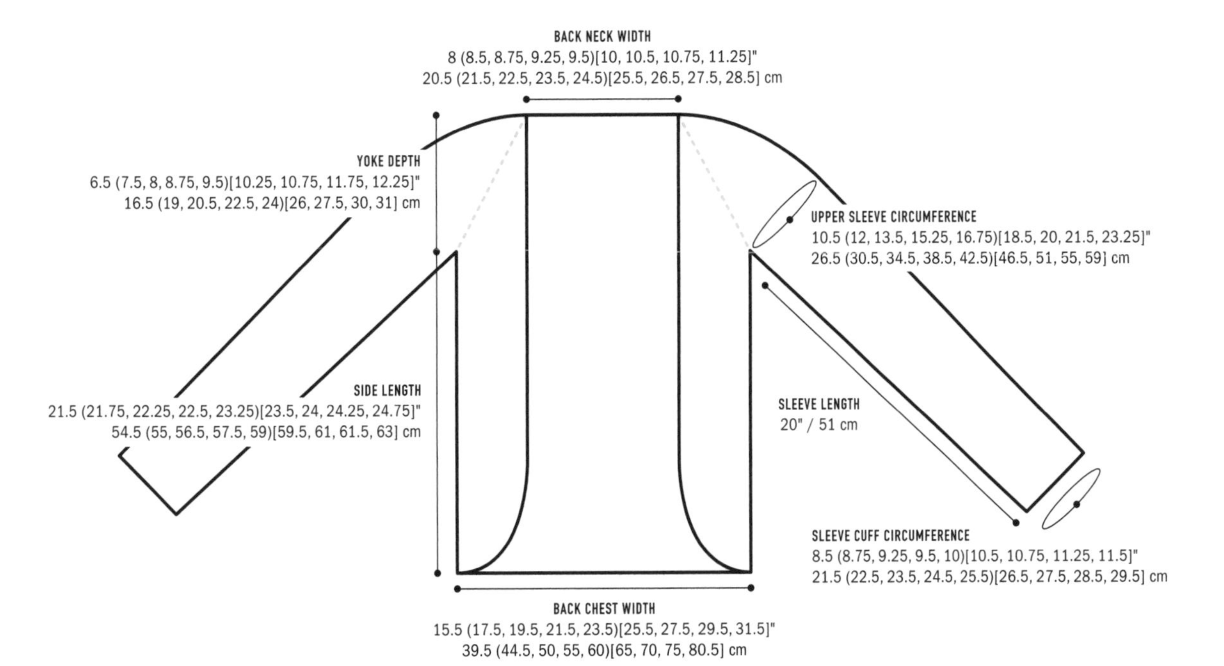
BACK NECK WIDTH
8 (8.5, 8.75, 9.25, 9.5)[10, 10.5, 10.75, 11.25]"
20.5 (21.5, 22.5, 23.5, 24.5)[25.5, 26.5, 27.5, 28.5] cm
YOKE DEPTH
6.5 (7.5, 8, 8.75, 9.5)[10.25, 10.75, 11.75, 12.25]"
16.5 (19, 20.5, 22.5, 24)[26, 27.5, 30, 31] cm
UPPER SLEEVE CIRCUMFERENCE
10.5 (12, 13.5, 15.25, 16.75)[18.5, 20, 21.5, 23.25]"
26.5 (30.5, 34.5, 38.5, 42.5)[46.5, 51, 55, 59] cm
SIDE LENGTH
21.5 (21.75, 22.25, 22.5, 23.25)[23.5, 24, 24.25, 24.75]"
54.5 (55, 56.5, 57.5, 59)[59.5, 61, 61.5, 63] cm
SLEEVE LENGTH
20" / 51 cm
SLEEVE CUFF CIRCUMFERENCE
8.5 (8.75, 9.25, 9.5, 10)[10.5, 10.75, 11.25, 11.5]"
21.5 (22.5, 23.5, 24.5, 25.5)[26.5, 27.5, 28.5, 29.5] cm
BACK CHEST WIDTH
15.5 (17.5, 19.5, 21.5, 23.5)[25.5, 27.5, 29.5, 31.5]"
39.5 (44.5, 50, 55, 60)[65, 70, 75, 80.5] cm

Side length measurement includes the 5" / 13 cm border.

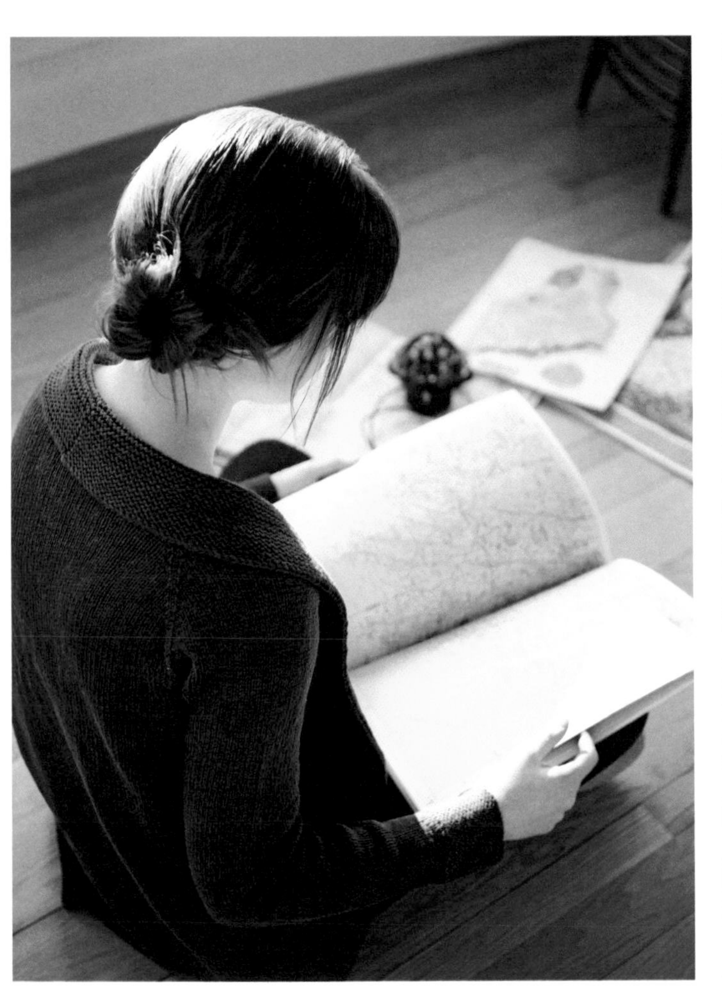

Cont in St st for 23 (14, 10, 8, 6)[5, 5, 4, 4] rnds.

DEC RND: K1, ssk, knit to last 3 sts of rnd, k2tog, k1. 2 sts dec.

Rep this dec rnd every 24 (15, 11, 9, 7)[6, 6, 5, 5] rnds 4 (7, 9, 7, 16)[19, 4, 15, 3] times, then every - (-, 10, 8, -)[-, 5, 4, 4) rnds - (-, 1, 6, -)[-, 18, 10, 25] time(s) more. 42 (44, 46, 48, 50)[52, 54, 56, 58] sts.

Cont in St st until sleeve meas 17" / 43 cm, or 3" / 7.5 cm shorter than desired length.

Work in garter st for 3" / 7.5 cm.

BO all sts.

FINISHING

COLLAR

With circular needle and beg at center back neck, pick up and knit 34 (35, 36, 37, 38)[39, 40, 41, 42] sts along neck edge, pick up and knit 2 sts for every 3 rows down left front including dec edge, pick up and knit 82 (92, 102, 114, 124)[134, 146, 156, 166] sts along bottom edge, pick up and knit 2 sts for every 3 rows up right front edge, pick up and knit 34 (35, 36, 37, 38)[39, 40, 41, 42] sts along neck edge to center back neck. Pm and join for working in the rnd.

Work in garter st for 5" / 12.5 cm, ending with a RS row.

BO all sts.

Weave in all ends. Block to measurements.

KNIT IN PIECES AND SEAMED

BACK

Using circular needle and a long-tail cast on, CO 80 (90, 100, 110, 120)[130, 140, 150, 160] sts. Do not join.

Beg with a WS row, work in St st until piece meas 16.5 (16.75, 17.25, 17.5, 18.25)[18.5, 19, 19.25, 19.75]" / 41.5 (42.5, 44, 44.5, 46)[47, 48.5, 49, 50.5] cm from CO edge, ending with a WS row.

SHAPE RAGLAN
BO 2 (3, 4, 5, 6)[7, 8, 9, 10] sts at beg of next 2 rows. 76 (84, 92, 100, 108)[116, 124, 132, 140] sts.

DEC ROW (RS): K2, ssk, knit to last 4 sts, k2tog, k2. 2 sts dec.

Rep dec row every 4 rows 5 (5, 4, 4, 3)[3, 2, 2, 1] time(s) more, then every RS row 11 (14, 18, 21, 25)[28, 32, 35, 39] times more. 42 (44, 46, 48, 50)[52, 54, 56, 58] sts.

Purl 1 WS row.

BO all sts.

LEFT FRONT
Using circular needle and a long-tail cast on, CO 2 sts.

Purl 1 WS row.

INC ROW (RS): Knit to last st, M1R, k1. 1 st inc.

Cont in St st, rep this inc row every RS row 17 (21, 25, 29, 33)[37, 41, 45, 49] times more, every 8 (8, 8, 6, 8)[6, 8, 6, 6] rows 5 (8, 5, 1, 5)[2, 5, 3, 1] time(s) more, then every 10 (-, 10, 8, 10)[8, -, 8, 8] rows 3 (-, 2, 6, 1)[4, -, 2, 3] time(s) more. 28 (32, 35, 39, 42)[46, 49, 53, 56] sts.

Work 7 rows in St st, ending with a WS row.

SHAPE RAGLAN
BO 2 (3, 4, 5, 6)[7, 8, 9, 10] sts, knit to end. 26 (29, 31, 34, 36)[39, 41, 44, 46] sts.

Purl 1 WS row.

DEC ROW (RS): K2, ssk, knit to end. 1 st dec.

Rep this dec row every RS row 21 (24, 26, 29, 31)[34, 36, 39, 41] times. 4 sts.

Purl 1 WS row.

BO all sts.

RIGHT FRONT
Using circular needle and a long-tail cast on, CO 2 sts.

Purl 1 WS row.

INC ROW (RS): K1, M1L, knit to end. 1 st inc.

Cont in St st, rep this inc row every RS row 17 (21, 25, 29, 33)[37, 41, 45, 49] times, every 8 (8, 8, 6, 8)[6, 8, 6, 6] rows 5 (8, 5, 1, 5)[2, 5, 3, 1] time(s) more, then every 10 (-, 10, 8, 10)[8, -, 8, 8] rows 3 (-, 2, 6, 1)[4, -, 2, 3] time(s) more. 28 (32, 35, 39, 42)[46, 49, 53, 56] sts.

Work 8 rows in St st, ending with a RS row.

SHAPE RAGLAN
BO 2 (3, 4, 5, 6)[7, 8, 9, 10] sts, purl to end. 26 (29, 31, 34, 36)[39, 41, 44, 46] sts.

DEC ROW (RS): Knit to last 4 sts, k2tog, k2. 1 st dec.

Rep this dec row every RS row 21 (24, 26, 29, 31)[34, 36, 39, 41] times more. 4 sts.

Purl 1 WS row.

BO all sts.

SLEEVES
Using circular needle and a long-tail cast on, CO 44 (46, 48, 50, 52)[54, 56, 58, 60] sts.

Work in garter st for 3" / 7.5 cm.

INC ROW (RS): K2, M1L, knit until 2 sts rem, M1R, k2. 2 sts inc.

Rep this inc row every 24 (14, 10, 8, 6)[6, 6, 6, 6] rows 4 (3, 5, 9, 8)[19, 13, 8, 2] times, then every - (16, 12, 10, 8)[-, 4, 4, 4] rows - (4, 5, 4, 8)[-, 9, 17, 26] times more. 54 (62, 70, 78, 86)[94, 102, 110, 118] sts.

Cont in St st until sleeve meas 20" / 51 cm, ending with a WS row.

SHAPE RAGLAN
BO 2 (3, 4, 5, 6)[7, 8, 9, 10] sts at beg of next 2 rows. 50 (56, 62, 68, 74)[80, 86, 92, 98] sts.

DEC ROW (RS): K2, ssk, knit to last 4 sts, k2tog, k2. 2 sts dec.

Rep this dec row every 4 rows 5 (5, 4, 4, 3)[3, 2, 2, 1] time(s) more, then every RS row 11 (14, 18, 21, 25)[28, 32, 35, 39] times more. 16 sts.

Purl 1 WS row.

BO all sts.

FINISHING
Seam raglan seams using a mattress stitch. Seam side and sleeve seams.

See seamless version for collar instructions.

Weave in all ends. Block to measurements.

MOTO JACKET

Moto Jacket *has ultimate versatility. It can be worn three different ways: swingy and open, partially buttoned with a wide collar, or buttoned up completely with a sculptural collar.*

The pictured sweater is knitted seamless from the top down. If you prefer seamed knits, a second set of instructions is included to knit the cardigan in pieces. This will yield the same result. For more on why you might choose one construction method over the other, *see page 40.* *In both versions, the collar, button band and buttonhole band are picked up and knitted last.*

If you are in-between sizes, I suggest sizing up for this design. When choosing your size it is always a good idea to check your actual body measurements against all the measurements given in the pattern schematic.

FINISHED MEASUREMENTS
Chest circumference: 33 (36, 39, 42, 45) [48, 51, 54, 57]" / 84 (91.5, 99, 106.5, 114.5)[122, 129.5, 137, 145] cm
Shown in size 33" / 84 cm with 0.5" / 1.5 cm of negative ease.

YARN
8 (9, 10, 10, 11)[12, 13, 14, 15] skeins Quince & Co. *Chickadee* (100% wool; 181 yd / 166 m per 50 g skein) in Storm

OR 1375 (1500, 1650, 1800, 1925)[2100, 2225, 2400, 2575] yd / 1250 (1375, 1500, 1625, 1750)[1900, 2050, 2200, 2350] m of dk weight yarn

NEEDLES
US 5 / 3.75 mm:
- 32" / 80 cm circular needle
- set of double-pointed needles

Or size needed to obtain gauge.

NOTIONS
Stitch markers, stitch holders or waste yarn, locking stitch markers, tapestry needle, 11 (11, 11, 11, 12)[12, 13, 13, 13] 0.5" / 13 mm buttons, sewing needle and thread

GAUGE
24 sts and 32 rows = 4" / 10 cm in St st

KNIT SEAMLESS FROM THE TOP DOWN

BEGIN AT TOP
Using circular needle and a long-tail cast on, CO 60 (62, 64, 66, 68)[70, 72, 74, 76] sts.

SETUP ROW (WS): P3, pm, p8, pm, p38 (40, 42, 44, 46)[48, 50, 52, 54], pm, p8, pm, p3.

ESTABLISH NECK AND RAGLAN INCREASES
ROW 1—NECK AND RAGLAN INC ROW(RS): K1, M1L, (knit to 1 st before m, M1R, k1, sm, k1, M1L) 4 times, knit to 1 st before end of row, M1R, k1. 10 sts inc.
ROW 2 (WS): Purl.
ROW 3—SLEEVE AND BACK ONLY INC ROW: Knit to m, sm, (k1, M1L, knit to 1 st before m, M1R, k1, sm) 3 times, knit to end. 6 sts inc.
ROW 4: Purl.

Rep rows 1–4 for 10 (11, 11, 12, 12)[13, 13, 14, 14] times more. 236 (254, 256, 274, 276) [294, 296, 314, 316] sts: 25 (27, 27, 29, 29)[31, 31, 33, 33] front sts, 52 (56, 56, 60, 60)[64, 64, 68, 68] sleeve sts, 82 (88, 90, 96, 98)[104, 106, 112, 114] back sts.

(RS): K1, M1L, (knit to 1 st before m, M1R, k1, sm, k1, M1L) rep 4 times, knit to 1 st before end of row, M1R, k1, then using a backward loop cast on, CO 23 (24, 26, 27, 29) [30, 32, 33, 35] sts.
(WS): Purl to end, then using a backward loop cast on, CO 23 (24, 26, 27, 29) [30, 32, 33, 35] sts. 292 (312, 318, 338, 344) [364, 370, 390, 396] sts.

ROW 1—SLEEVE AND BACK ONLY INC ROW: Knit to m, sm, (K1, M1L, knit to 1 st before m, M1R, k1, sm) 3 times, knit to end. 6 sts inc.
ROW 2: Purl.
ROW 3—RAGLAN INC ROW (RS): (Knit to 1 st before m, M1R, k1, sm, k1, M1L) 4 times, knit to end. 8 sts inc.
ROW 4 (WS): Purl.

Rep rows 1–4 for 1 (1, 2, 2, 3)[3, 4, 4, 5] time(s), then work rows 1 & 2 once more. 326 (346, 366, 386, 406)[426, 446, 466, 486] sts: 52 (55, 58, 61, 64)[67, 70, 73, 76] front sts, 64 (68, 72, 76, 80)[84, 88, 92, 96] sleeve sts, 94 (100, 106, 112, 118) [124, 130, 136, 142] back sts.

DIVIDE SLEEVES FROM BODY
(Removing markers as you go, knit to m, place 64 (68, 72, 76, 80)[84, 88, 92, 96] sleeve sts on a stitch holder, using a backward loop cast on, CO 5 (8, 11, 14, 17)[20, 23, 26, 29] underarm sts) twice, knit to end. 208 (226, 244, 262, 280) [298, 316, 334, 352] sts.

Work in St st for 3 rows.

NECK EDGE DEC ROW (RS): K1, ssk, knit to 3 sts before end of row, k2tog, k1. 2 sts dec.

Rep this dec row every 4th row 5 times more. 196 (214, 232, 250, 268)[286, 304, 322, 340] sts.

Cont in St st until body meas 9.5 (10, 10.25, 10.75, 11)[11.5, 11.75, 12.25, 12.5]" / 24 (25.5, 26, 27.5, 28)[29, 30, 31, 32] cm or 3" / 7.5 cm shorter than desired length.

Work in garter st until body meas 12.5 (13, 13.25, 13.75, 14) [14.5, 14.75, 15.25, 15.5]" / 32 (33, 33.5, 35, 35.5)[37, 37.5, 38.5, 39.5] cm.

BO all sts.

SLEEVES

Divide 64 (68, 72, 76, 80)[84, 88, 92, 96] held sleeve sts evenly over 3 dpns. With a 4th dpn, pick up and knit 5 (8, 11, 14, 17) [20, 23, 26, 29] sts from underarm edge and pm in center of picked up sts to mark beg of rnd. Join for working in the rnd, knit to m. 69 (76, 83, 90, 97)[104, 111, 118, 125] sts.

Work in St st for 18 (11, 9, 7, 6)[5, 4, 4, 3] rnds.

DEC RND: K1, ssk, knit to last 3 sts, k2tog, k1. 2 sts dec.

Work dec rnd every 19 (12, 10, 8, 7)[6, 5, 5, 4) rnds 4 (7, 2, 12, 7)[13, 19, 11, 25] times more, then every 0 (0, 9, 0, 6)[5, 4, 4, 0] rnds 0 (0, 8, 0, 8)[4, 1, 11, 0] time(s) more. 59 (60, 61, 64, 65)[68, 69, 72, 73] sts.

Cont in St st until sleeve meas 15" / 38 cm from underarm edge or 3" / 7.5 cm shorter than desired length.

Work in garter st until sleeve meas 18" / 45.5 cm, ending with a RS row.

BO all sts.

FINISHING

COLLAR

With RS facing, beg at neck edge at top of right front, pick up and knit 23 (24, 26, 27, 29) [30, 32, 33, 35] sts along cast-on sts on right front, 2 sts for every 3 rows along slanted neck edge, 60 (62, 64, 66, 68)[70, 72, 74, 76] sts along original cast-on sts, 2 sts for every 3 rows along slanted neck edge, and 23 (24, 26, 27, 29)[30, 32, 33, 35] sts along cast-on sts on left front.

Work in St st until collar meas 6" / 15 cm or 1" / 2.5 cm shorter than desired length.

Work in garter st for 1" / 2.5 cm, ending with a RS row.

BO all sts.

BUTTON BAND

With circular needle, RS facing and starting at the neck edge of the left front center, pick up and knit 2 sts for every 3 rows along left front edge, continuing to lower edge.

Work in garter st for 8 rows, ending with a RS row.

BO all sts.

BUTTONHOLE BAND

With circular needle, RS facing and starting at the lower edge of the right front center, pick up and knit 2 sts for every 3 rows along right front edge, continuing to top of collar.

Work in garter st for 3 rows.

Attach 11 (11, 11, 11, 12)[12, 13, 13, 13] locking stitch markers to the button band to mark button locations, one 0.5" / 1.5 cm from the top, one 1.5" / 4 cm from the bottom, and the rest spaced evenly between.

BUTTONHOLE ROW (RS): (Knit to m, work double yo buttonhole [see page 77])11 (11, 11, 11, 12)[12, 13, 13, 13] times, knit to end.

Cont in garter st for 4 rows.

BO all sts.

Weave in ends. Block to measurements.

Lay sweater out with right front crossed over left front. Attach buttons underneath buttonholes.

KNIT IN PIECES AND SEAMED

BACK

Using circular needle, CO 102 (110, 120, 128, 138)[146, 156, 164, 174] sts.

Work in garter st until piece meas 3" / 7.5 cm from CO edge.

Cont in St st until piece meas 12.5 (13.5, 14, 14.5, 15)[15.5, 16, 16.5, 17]" / 32 (33, 33.5, 35, 35.5)[37, 37.5, 38.5, 39.5] cm from CO edge, ending with a WS row.

SHAPE RAGLAN

BO 3 (4, 6, 7, 9)[10, 12, 13, 15] sts at beg of next 2 rows. 96 (102, 108, 114, 120)[126, 132, 138, 144] sts.

DEC ROW (RS): K2, ssk, knit to 4 sts before end of row, k2tog, k2. 2 sts dec.

Work dec row every RS row 27 (29, 31, 33, 35)[37, 39, 41, 43] times more. 40 (42, 44, 46, 48)[50, 52, 54, 56] sts.

Purl 1 WS row.

BO all sts.

LEFT FRONT

Using circular needle, CO 50 (54, 59, 63, 68)[72, 77, 81, 86] sts.

Work in garter st until piece meas 3" / 7.5 cm from CO edge.

Cont in St st until body meas 9.5 (10, 10.25, 10.75, 11)[11.5, 11.75, 12.25, 12.5]" / 24 (25.5, 26, 27.5, 28)[29, 30, 31, 32] cm, ending with a WS row.

NECK EDGE INC ROW (RS): Knit to 3 sts before end of row, M1R, k1. 1 st inc.

Rep this inc row every 4th row 5 times more. 56 (60, 65, 69, 74)[78, 83, 87, 92]

Work in St st for 3 rows.

SHAPE RAGLAN

BO 3 (4, 6, 7, 9)[10, 12, 13, 15] sts, knit to end. 53 (56, 59, 62, 65)[68, 71, 74, 77] sts.

Work in St st for 3 rows.

DEC ROW (RS): K2, ssk, knit to end. 1 st dec.

Rep dec row every 4th row 1 (1, 2, 2, 3)[3, 4, 4, 5] time(s). 51 (54, 56, 59, 61)[64, 66, 69, 71] sts.

Purl 1 WS row.

(RS): K2, ssk, k22 (24, 24, 26, 26)[28, 28, 30, 30], k2tog, knit to end.
(WS): BO 23 (24, 26, 27, 29) [30, 32, 33, 35] sts, purl to end. 26 (28, 28, 30, 30)[32, 32, 34, 34] sts.

Work in St st for 2 rows.

DEC ROW (RS): K2, ssk, knit to 3 sts before end of row, k2tog, k1. 2 sts dec.

Rep this dec row every 4th row 10 (11, 11, 12, 12)[13, 13, 14, 14] times more. 4 sts.

Purl 1 WS row.

BO all sts.

RIGHT FRONT

CO 50 (54, 59, 63, 68)[72, 77, 81, 86] sts.

Work in garter st until piece meas 3" / 7.5 cm from CO edge.

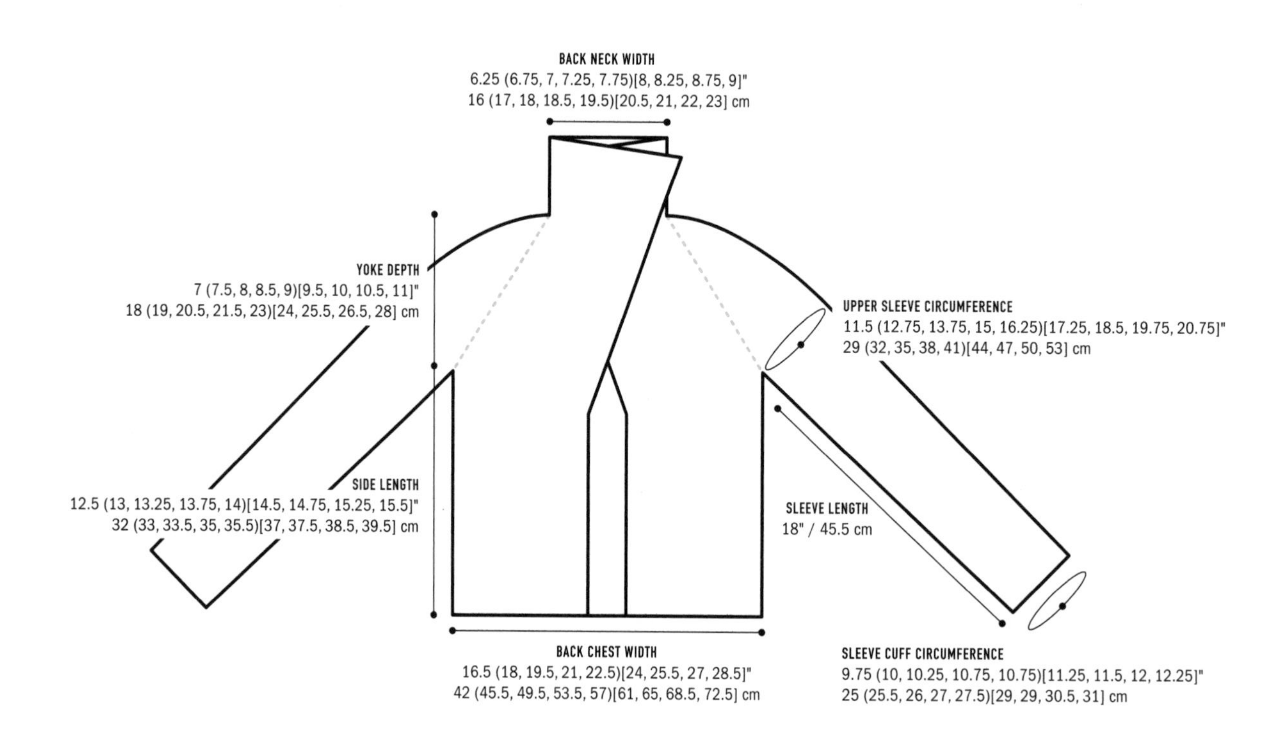

Cont in St st until body meas 9.5 (10, 10.25, 10.75, 11)[11.5, 11.75, 12.25, 12.5]" / 24 (25.5, 26, 27.5, 28)[29, 30, 31, 32] cm, ending with a WS row.

NECK EDGE INC ROW (RS): K1, M1L, knit to end. 1 st inc.

Rep this inc row every 4th row 5 times more. 56 (60, 65, 69, 74)[78, 83, 87, 92] sts.

Work in St st for 4 rows.

SHAPE RAGLAN
BO 3 (4, 6, 7, 9)[10, 12, 13, 15] sts, purl to end. 53 (56, 59, 62, 65)[68, 71, 74, 77] sts.

Work in St st for 2 rows.

DEC ROW (RS): Knit to 4 sts before end of row, k2tog, k2. 1 st dec.

Rep this dec row every 4th row 1 (1, 2, 2, 3)[3, 4, 4, 5] time(s). 51 (54, 56, 59, 61)[64, 66, 69, 71] sts.

Purl 1 WS row.

(RS): BO 23 (24, 26, 27, 29) [30, 32, 33, 35] sts, k1, ssk, knit to 4 sts before end of row, k2tog, k2. 26 (28, 28, 30, 30)[32, 32, 34, 34] sts.

Work in St st for 3 rows.

DEC ROW (RS): K2, ssk, knit to 3 sts before end of row, k2tog, k1. 2 sts dec.

Rep this dec row every 4th row 10 (11, 11, 12, 12)[13, 13, 14, 14] times more. 4 sts.

Purl 1 WS row.

BO all sts.

SLEEVES

Using circular needle, CO 62 (62, 64, 66, 68)[70, 72, 74, 76] sts.

Work in garter st for 3" / 7.5 cm, ending with a WS row.

Work in St st for 4 rows.

INC ROW (RS): K2, M1L, knit to 2 sts before end of row, M1R, k2. 2 sts inc.

Rep this inc row every 18 (12, 10, 8, 8)[6, 6, 6, 4] rows 4 (7, 6, 12, 3)[15, 9, 5, 25] times more, then every - (-, 8, -, 6)[4, 4, 4, -] rows - (-, 4, -, 12)[2, 11, 17, -] times more. 72 (78, 86, 92, 100) [106, 114, 120, 128] sts.

Cont in St st until sleeve meas 18" / 45.5 cm, ending with a WS row.

SHAPE RAGLAN
BO 3 (4, 6, 7, 9)[10, 12, 13, 15] sts at beg of next 2 rows. 66 (70, 74, 78, 82)[86, 90, 94, 98] sts.

DEC ROW (RS): K2, ssk, knit to 4 sts before end of row, k2tog, k2. 2 sts dec.

Rep this dec row every RS row 27 (29, 31, 33, 35)[37, 39, 41, 43] times more. 10 sts.

Purl 1 WS row.

BO all sts.

FINISHING
Seam raglan seams. Seam side and sleeve seams.

See seamless version for collar, button band and buttonhole band instructions.

Weave in ends. Block to measurements.

Lay sweater out with right front crossed over left front. Attach buttons underneath buttonholes.

KNITTING IN THE ROUND

DOUBLE-POINTED NEEDLES METHOD

I find this method to be the least fussy. However, you are the most likely to have "ladders" in your sleeve where the needles join, especially if you're knitting at a looser gauge. With this in mind, when knitting in the round with dpns be sure to pull the yarn tight at the beginning and end of each needle.

HOW TO DO IT

Divide your stitches evenly over 3 or 4 dpns. Join for working in the round. With a 4th or 5th dpn, knit to the end of needle 1, being sure to pull your yarn tight at the join at the end of the needle. With the newly emptied dpn, knit to the end of needle 2. Continue around.

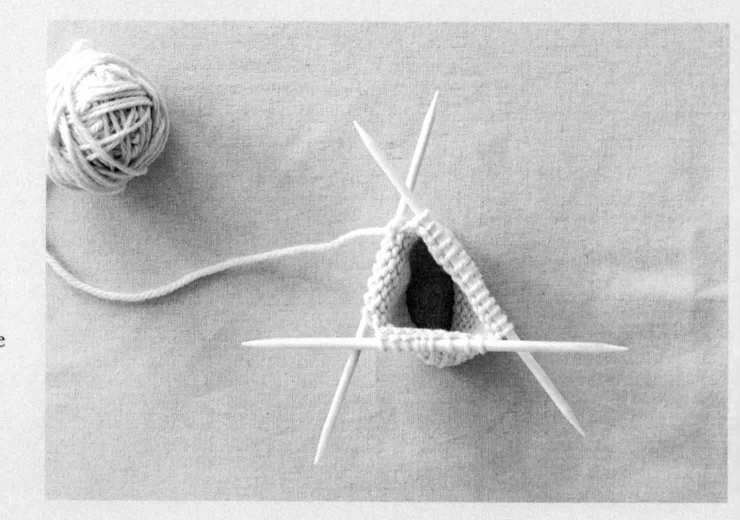

TWO CIRCULAR NEEDLES METHOD

I was first turned on to this method when I took a sock class with Cat Bordhi. It is my favorite. You have fewer joins between needles compared to using double-pointed needles and I find it easier to pull the yarn tight at these joins, avoiding the unwanted "ladder" effect. It can feel a little time consuming to switch back and forth between the two needles.

HOW TO DO IT

Divide stitches evenly between two circular needles. With working yarn hanging to the right, slide stitches on the front circular needle to right needle tip and knit the stitches with the left needle tip from the same circular needle. Once you've knit all stitches, turn your work and slide all stitches to the right needle tip of the 2nd circular needle. Knit all the stitches on the 2nd circular needle with the left needle tip of the 2nd circular needle. Continue around.

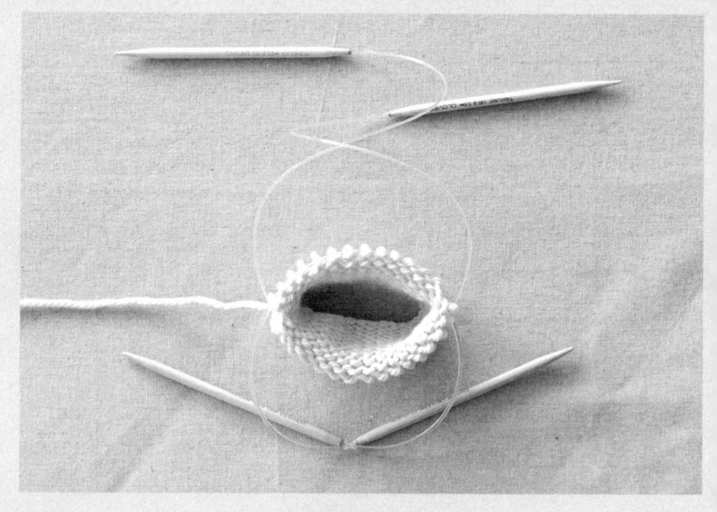

***MAGIC LOOP* METHOD**

I'll admit, I only first tried *Magic Loop* a year ago. Sometimes I find it fussy to move the cable back and forth, but the results are very good.

HOW TO DO IT

You'll need a circular needle with a cable that is at least 32" / 80 cm long. Once your stitches are on the needles, divide them in half, bend the cable, and pull it out between the divided stitches. Slide the stitches down to the needle tips. Your needle tips should point right and be parallel, with your working yarn hanging in the back. Pull the back needle out, leaving enough cable to allow you to knit with the needle tip. Knit all of the stitches on the front needle, being careful that you haven't twisted the stitches. Once you've knit all stitches from the front needle, slide both sets of stitches down to their needle tips. With your needle tips once again pointing right and parallel, pull the back needle tip out leaving enough cable to allow you to knit with the needle tip. Continue around.

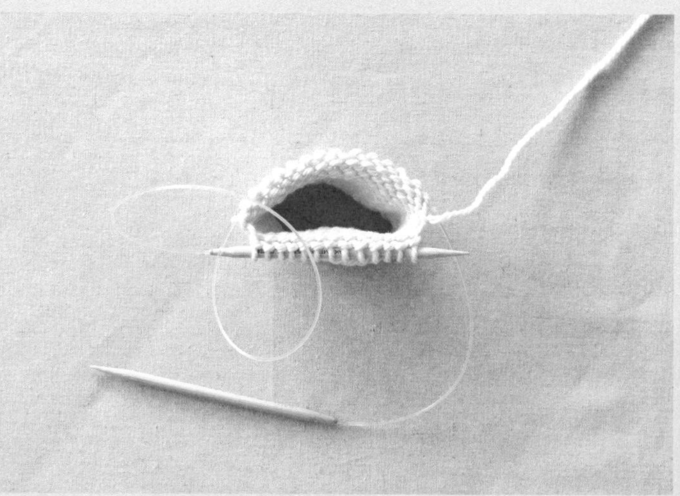

BUTTON BANDS & BUTTONHOLES

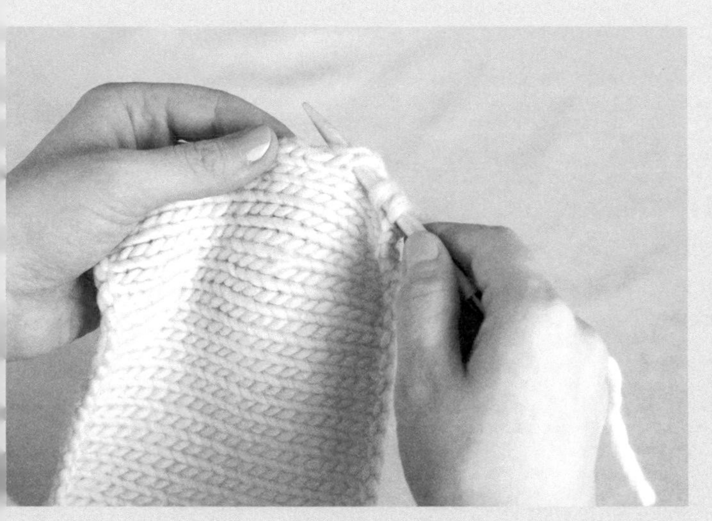

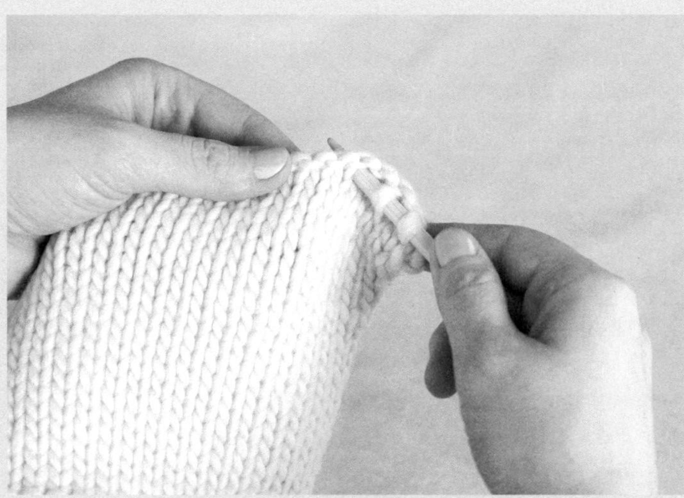

PICKING UP ALONG A VERTICAL EDGE

If you pull your knit fabric apart you'll notice little bars running horizontally between stitches. There are little "windows" of space between these bars, and this is where you want to pick up and knit along a vertical edge. Moving in one whole stitch from the edge, insert your left needle through the first window and knit a stitch onto your right needle. The pattern should tell you what rate to pick up, whether it's 2 stitches for every 3 rows or 3 stitches for every 4 rows. In the case of 3 stitches for every 4 rows, you would pick up and knit through 3 windows in a row, then skip the 4th window. The same could apply for picking up along a slanted edge, but depending on your gauge you may find you need to pick up every row for neatness' sake.

PICKING UP ALONG A HORIZONTAL EDGE

When you're picking up on a horizontal edge it's either a cast on or a bound off edge. You insert your left needle under each cast on or bound off stitch and knit one stitch onto your right needle. Your ratio is stitch for stitch. Be careful to pick up under an entire stitch, not half a stitch.

TIP | Use your swatch to practice picking up and knitting bands. When knitting your swatch, work in a few buttonholes to see how they'll look.

ONE-ROW BUTTONHOLE

This 5-st one-row buttonhole is used in *Calligraphy* (page 44).

Step 1: Bring yarn to front, sl 1 st from left to right needle, move yarn to back, sl 1 st from right to left needle. Pass second st on left needle over first st. Repeat 4 times more, for a total of 5 sts bound off. Sl last st back to left needle. Turn work so WS is facing.

Step 2: Using knitted cast on, CO 6 sts, which is 1 st more than bound off, onto your left needle. Turn work so that the RS is facing once again.

Step 3: Slip 1 st from left needle to right needle. Pass second st on right needle over first st.

DOUBLE YO, AKA PAM ALLEN'S FAVORITE BUTTONHOLE

This buttonhole is used in *Moto Jacket* (page 68).

(RS): Work to 2 sts before the buttonhole st and make a double yo by bringing the yarn through the needles to the front, then over the RH needle to the back, then to the front between the needles again. Knit the next 2 sts together, work to end of row.

(WS): Work to the yo, purl into the yarn over, letting the second wrap drop from the left needle, work to end of row.

(RS): Work to the st above the buttonhole, knit into the hole (not the stitch above) and work to end.

HOW TO SPACE BUTTONHOLES

Pick up and knit your button band first. Gather as many locking stitch markers or safety pins as you have buttons. Place a marker 0.5–2" / 1.5–5 cm from top edge (depending on button size) and 1.5–2.5" / 4–6.5 cm from bottom edge. Mark where the buttonhole's center will be. Evenly space the remaining markers between these first two. You can measure them out perfectly; I just eyeball it.

FINISHING

Why finish your knits properly? If you're especially drawn to top down seamless raglans, you may have an aversion to any sort of finishing. But even in the case of these sweaters, taking the time to learn to weave in ends and block properly will go a long way toward giving your sweater a beautifully finished appearance.

WEAVING IN ENDS

When you start and finish knitting with a skein of yarn, you'll be left with a tail of yarn hanging off the back of your fabric. What to do with these tails? First of all, do yourself a favor and start and end skeins in easy-to-conceal places. If you're knitting flat pieces, always start or finish a skein at the beginning or end of a row. If you're knitting in the round or seamlessly, start or finish a skein where a seam would be: at the side, under the arm, or near a raglan line. There are many ways to weave in an end. However you choose to do it, you should weave it in, not tie it off in a knot. Once blocked, the fibers will meld together for good (especially if you're using animal fibers). You can practice weaving in ends on your swatch. Use a different color yarn so you can see what you're doing. I like to trace the path of the yarn along its journey to create stitches. There are many video tutorials on line available for weaving in ends, or you can consult your favorite A-to-Z how-to-knit book.

BLOCKING

We talked about blocking in our discussion on gauge and swatches on page 28. Now let's talk about our finished garment. You have the same options—you can either take a steam iron to it or wet block.

My initial blocking of a garment is always a wet block, then for future touch ups I'll use a steam iron. After I've soaked my garment and squeezed out the water... Well, honestly, first I smell it. It smells so good! Then I lay it out on my blocking board (a sea of towels works just as well). Now the fun part: you can start manipulating the damp fabric. Referring to your schematic, you can stretch and smooth your garment to match the measurements for your size. The advantage of a blocking board is that you can pin your sweater into place. This is especially nice when you've knit in a lace pattern. For the Stockinette stitch fabric featured in this book you'll be fine with towels.

Now we play the waiting game: depending on the time of year it can take up to a few days for your sweater to completely dry. I have to keep shooing the cat off the board and readjusting—it's all part of the fun.

If you've never blocked a sweater before, you will be amazed once yours is dry. Most knitting sins have been erased and you're left with a beautifully even fabric that is the size and shape you wanted it to be! One note of caution: use care when blocking ribbing and don't over-stretch it. You want those borders to maintain their elasticity. When knitting seamed sweaters, I like to block the individual pieces before seaming. After blocking, the pieces lay flat and are easier to seam.

If this has been your first sweater knitting experience, I do hope you felt supported through the additional content in this book! If it didn't turn out perfectly, please don't be discouraged. Focus on what you learned and how this will help you when you knit your next sweater!

SYCAMORE

A minimalist vest acts like an accessory, adding some punch to an everyday outfit.

Sycamore *is knitted seamlessly from the bottom up until you divide for the armholes. Charted borders are worked at the same time. The back and fronts are then worked separately. The collar and armholes are picked up and knitted.*

For this pattern you'll be knitting both from written instructions and from charts. When knitting from charts, read them from right to left on the right side (RS) or odd rows, and from left to right when knitting on the wrong side (WS) or even rows.

FINISHED MEASUREMENTS

Chest circumference: 32.75 (36, 39.25, 42.75, 46)" / 83 (91.5, 100, 108.5, 117) cm

Shown in size 32.75" / 83 cm with no ease.

YARN

4 (5, 6, 6, 7) skeins Quince & Co. *Chickadee* (100% wool; 181 yd / 166 m per 50 g skein) in Chanterelle

OR 725 (825, 925, 1025, 1150) yd / 650 (750, 850, 950, 1050) m of dk weight yarn

NEEDLES

US 5 / 3.75 mm:

- 32" / 80 cm circular needle
- 16" / 40 cm circular needle

Or size needed to obtain gauge.

NOTIONS

Stitch markers, stitch holders or waste yarn, tapestry needle

GAUGE

24 sts and 32 rows = 4" / 10 cm in St st

BODY

Using longer circular needle and a long-tail cast on, CO 220 (240, 260, 280, 300) sts.

SETUP ROW (RS): Work Chart A 22 (24, 26, 28, 30) times, pm (center back), work Chart B 22 (24, 26, 28, 30) times.
(WS): Work Chart B to m, sm, work Chart A to end.

Cont as est, working rows 3–10 of charts, then work rows 1–6 of charts once more.

On last row, remove center back marker and place new markers as follows: Work Chart B twice, pm, work 51 (56, 61, 66, 71) sts, pm (side marker), work 98 (108, 118, 128, 138) sts, removing center back marker and switching to Chart A as est, pm (side marker), work to last 10 sts, pm, work to end of row.

ROW 1—DEC ROW (RS): Work Chart A twice, (knit to 3 sts before side m, k2tog, k1, sm, k1, ssk) twice, knit to m, work Chart B twice. 4 sts dec.
ROW 2 (WS): Work Chart B twice, purl to last 10 sts, work Chart A twice.

Cont as est, AT THE SAME TIME, rep dec row every 14 (16, 18, 20, 22) rows twice. 208 (228, 248, 268, 288) sts.

Cont as est for 7 rows.

INC ROW (RS): Work Chart A twice, (knit to 1 st before side m, M1R, k1, sm, k1, M1L) twice, knit to m, work Chart B twice. 4 sts inc.

Rep inc row every 16th row 2 times more. 220 (240, 260, 280, 300) sts.

Cont as est until piece meas 12.5 (13, 13.5, 14, 14.5)" / 32 (33, 34.5, 35.5, 37) cm from CO edge, ending with a WS row.

DIVIDE FOR ARMHOLES

(Work to 3 (4, 5, 6, 7) sts before side m, BO 6 (8, 10, 12, 14) underarm sts, removing side m) twice, work to end. Place 58 (62, 66, 70, 74) right front sts and 92 (100, 108, 116, 124) back sts onto stitch holders.

LEFT FRONT

(WS): Work Chart B twice, purl to end.

DEC ROW (RS): K1, ssk, work to end. 1 st dec.

Rep this dec row EOR 3 (4, 5, 6, 7) times more, then every 4th row once. 53 (56, 59, 62, 65) sts.

Work 3 rows even, ending with a WS row.

SHAPE NECK

K36 (38, 40, 42, 44), place rem 17 (18, 19, 20, 21) sts on a stitch holder.

Purl 1 WS row.

DEC ROW (RS): Knit to last 3 sts, k2tog, k1. 1 st dec.

Rep this dec row EOR 22 (23, 24, 25, 26) times more. 13 (14, 15, 16, 17) sts.

Purl 1 WS row.

SHAPE SHOULDER
BO 6 (7, 7, 8, 8) sts, knit to end.

Purl 1 WS row.

BO rem 7 (7, 8, 8, 9) sts.

RIGHT FRONT

Take 58 (62, 66, 70, 74) right front sts from holder and place them on needle, ready to work a WS row.

(WS): Purl to last 10 sts, work Chart A twice.
DEC ROW (RS): Knit to last 3 sts, k2tog, k1. 1 st dec.

Rep this dec row EOR 3 (4, 5, 6, 7) times more, then every 4th row once. 53 (56, 69, 62, 65) sts.

Work 3 rows even, ending with a WS row. Break yarn.

SHAPE NECK
Turn work, ready to work a RS row. Place first 17 (18, 19, 20, 21) sts on a stitch holder. Rejoin yarn and k36 (38, 40, 42, 44).

Purl 1 WS row.

DEC ROW (RS): K1, ssk, knit to end. 1 st dec.

Rep this dec row EOR 22 (23, 24, 25, 26) times more. 13 (14, 15, 16, 17) sts.

BO 6 (7, 7, 8, 8) sts, purl to end.

Knit 1 RS row.

BO rem 7 (7, 8, 8, 9) sts.

BACK

Place 92 (100, 108, 116, 124) back sts from stitch holder onto needle, ready to work a WS row.

Purl 1 WS row.

DEC ROW (RS): K1, ssk, knit to last 3 sts, k2tog, k1. 2 sts dec.

Rep this dec row EOR 3 (4, 5, 6, 7) times more, then every 4th row 9 times. 66 (72, 78, 84, 90) sts.

Cont in St st for 5 (7, 9, 11, 13) rows.

INC ROW (RS): K1, M1L, knit to last st, M1R, k1. 2 sts inc.

Rep this inc row EOR 4 times more. 76 (82, 88, 94, 100) sts.

Purl 1 WS row.

(RS): K1, M1L, k11 (12, 13, 14, 15), place previous 13 (14, 15, 16, 17) sts on a stitch holder for right shoulder, k52 (56, 60, 64, 68) then place these sts on a another stitch holder for the neck, k11 (12, 13, 14, 15), M1R, k1. 2 sts inc.

LEFT SHOULDER
ROW 1 (WS): Purl.
ROW 2 (RS): K1, ssk, knit to last st, M1R, k1.

Rep these 2 rows once more.

BO 6 (7, 7, 8, 8) sts, purl to end.

Knit 1 RS row.

BO rem 7 (7, 8, 8, 9) sts.

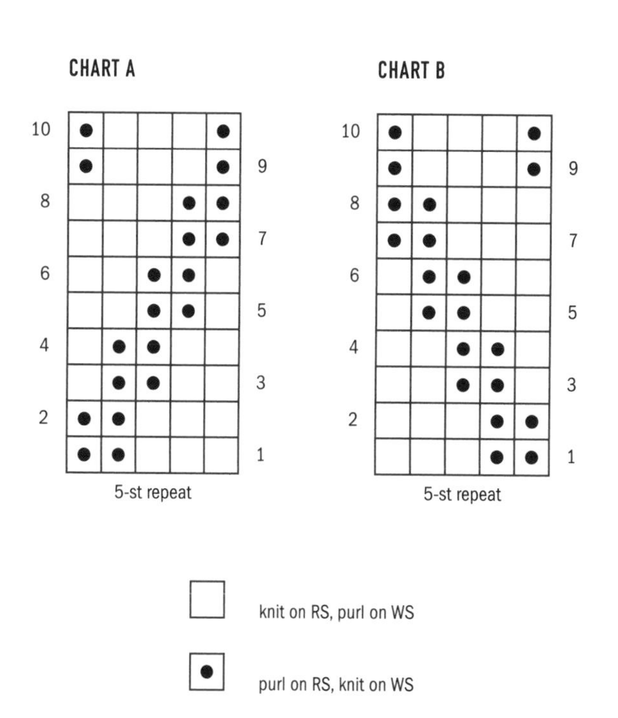

RIGHT SHOULDER

Place 13 (14, 15, 16, 17) right shoulder sts back on needle, ready to work a WS row.

ROW 1 (WS): Purl.

ROW 2 (RS): K1, M1L, knit to last 3 sts, k2tog, k1.

Rep these 2 rows once more.

Purl 1 WS row.

BO 6 (7, 7, 8, 8) sts, knit to end.

Purl 1 WS row.

BO rem 7 (7, 8, 8, 9) sts.

FINISHING

Seam shoulders.

COLLAR

Place 17 (18, 19, 20, 21) sts on hold from each front onto needle, ready to work a RS row. Work Row 7 (3, 9, 5, 1) of Chart A over first 10 sts, k7 (8, 9 10, 11), pick up and k22 (24, 26, 28, 25) sts along right neck edge, k26 (28, 30, 32, 34) back neck sts, pm (center back), k26 (28, 30, 32, 34) back neck sts, pick up and k22 (24, 26, 28, 25) sts along left neck edge, k7 (8, 9, 10, 11), work Row 7 (3, 9, 5, 1) of Chart B over last 10 sts. 130 (140, 150, 160, 160) sts.

(WS): Work Chart B as est over 10 sts, purl to last 10 sts, work Chart A as est to end.

(RS): Work Chart A 13 (14, 15, 16, 16) times, sm, work Chart B 13 (14, 15, 16, 16) times.

Cont as est 15 rows more.

BO all sts in patt.

ARMHOLES

With shorter circular needle and RS facing, pick up and knit 6 (8, 10, 12, 14) sts along underarm edge, then pick up and knit 2 sts for every 3 rows around the circumference of the armhole. Join for working in the rnd.

Knit 4 rnds.

BO loosely.

Weave in all ends. Block to measurements.

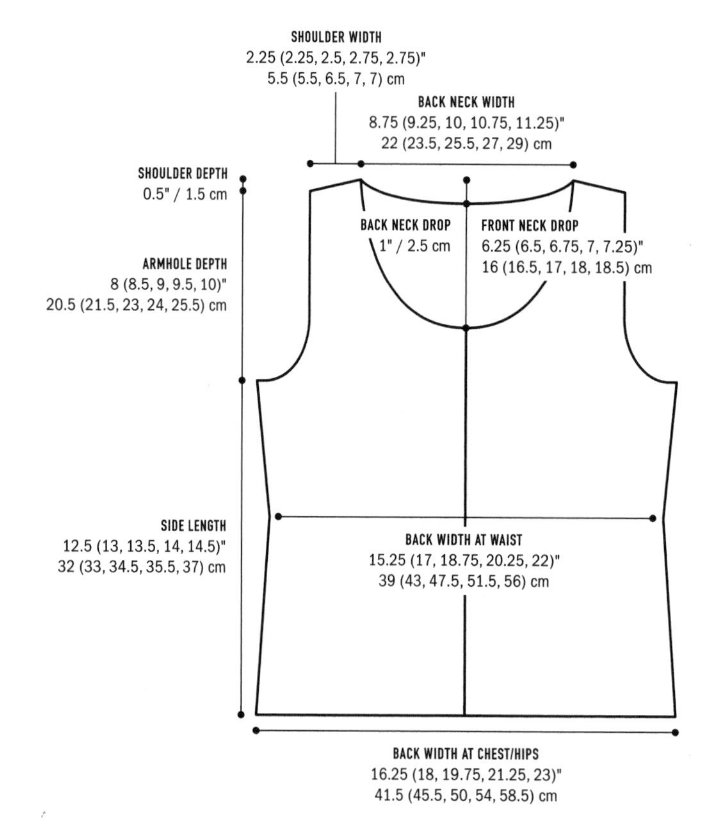

LESLEY

With a graceful neck fashioned with short rows, Lesley *lends itself well to a closer fit. Knitted in a loosely spun aran weight yarn, it's a comfortable pullover suitable for both indoor and outdoor adventures.*

The pictured sweater is knitted seamless from the top down. If you prefer seamed knits, a second set of instructions is included to knit the pullover in pieces. This will yield the same result. For more on why you might choose one construction method over the other, see page 40. In both versions, the collar is picked up and knitted last.

If you are in-between sizes, I suggest sizing down for a more fitted pullover. When choosing your size it is always a good idea to check your actual body measurements against all the measurements given in the pattern schematic.

FINISHED MEASUREMENTS

Chest circumference: 32 (36, 40, 44)[48, 52, 56, 60]" / 81.5 (91.5, 101.5, 112)[122, 132, 142, 152.5] cm

Shown in size 32" / 81.5 cm with 0.5" / 1.5 cm of negative ease.

YARN

4 (5, 5, 6)[6, 7, 7, 8] skeins Quince & Co. *Osprey* (100% wool; 170 yd / 155 m per 100 g skein) in Petal

OR 650 (725, 825, 900)[1000, 1075, 1175, 1275] yd / 600 (675, 750, 825)[900, 975, 1075, 1150] m of an aran weight yarn

NEEDLES

US 9 / 5.5 mm:

- 16" / 40 cm circular needle
- 32" / 80 cm circular needle
- set of double-pointed needles

US 10 / 6 mm:

- 16" / 40 cm circular needle
- 32" / 80 cm circular needle
- set of double-pointed needles

Or size needed to obtain gauge.

NOTIONS

Stitch markers, stitch holders or waste yarn, tapestry needle

GAUGE

14 sts and 20 rows = 4" / 10 cm in St st using larger needles

KNIT SEAMLESS FROM THE TOP DOWN

BEGIN AT TOP

With smaller circular needle and using the long-tail cast on, CO 86 (88, 90, 92)[94, 96, 98, 100] sts. Join for working in the rnd, being careful to not twist sts and pm to mark beg of rnd.

RIBBING SETUP RND: (K1, p1) rep to end.

Rep this rnd 7 times more.

Switch to larger circular needle.

SETUP RND: K24 (25, 26, 27)[28, 29, 30, 31] front sts, pm, k19 sleeve sts, pm, k24 (25, 26, 27)[28, 29, 30, 31] back sts, pm, k19 sleeve sts.

SHAPE NECK

SHORT ROW 1: K3, w&t.
SHORT ROW 2: Purl to 4th m, p3, w&t.
SHORT ROW 3: Knit to 2 sts past first wrapped st, knitting wrap together with wrapped st as you come to it, w&t.
SHORT ROW 4: Purl to 2 sts past 2nd wrapped st, purling wrap together with wrapped st as you come to it, w&t.

Knit to beg of rnd.

ESTABLISH NECK AND RAGLAN INCREASES

INC RND: (K1, M1L, knit to 1 st before m, M1R, k1) 4 times, knitting wraps together with wrapped sts as you come to them. 8 sts inc.

Rep this inc rnd every 4th rnd twice more, then every other rnd 0 (0, 2, 2)[4, 4, 6, 6] times more. 110 (112, 130, 132)[150, 152, 170, 172] sts: 30 (31, 36, 37)[42, 43, 48, 49] front/back sts, 25 (25, 29, 29)[33, 33, 37, 37] sleeve sts.

Knit 1 rnd.

RND 1—BODY ONLY INC RND: (K1, M1L, knit to 1 st before m, M1R, k1, sm, knit to m, sm) twice. 4 sts inc.
RND 2: Knit.
RND 3—SLEEVE AND BODY INC RND: (K1, M1L, knit to 1 st from m, M1R, k1) 4 times. 8 sts inc.
RND 4: Knit.

Rep these 4 rnds 4 (5, 5, 6)[6, 7, 7, 8] times more, then rep rnds 1 and 2 once more. 174 (188, 206, 220)[238, 252, 270, 284] sts: 52 (57, 62, 67)[72, 77, 82, 87] front/back sts, 35 (37, 41, 43)[47, 49, 53, 55] sleeve sts.

DIVIDE SLEEVES FROM BODY

(Removing markers, knit to m, place 35 (37, 41, 43)[47, 49, 53, 55] sleeve sts on a stitch holder, CO 4 (6, 8, 10)[12, 14, 16, 18] underarm sts using a backward loop cast on) twice, pm at center of last set of underarm sts for new beg of rnd. 112 (126, 140, 154)[168, 182, 196, 210] sts.

Cont working in the rnd in St st until body meas 12" / 30.5 cm from underarm.

Switch to smaller circular needle.

RIBBING SETUP RND: (K1, p1) rep to end of rnd.

Cont in ribbing as est for 3" / 7.5 cm.

BO all sts in ribbing.

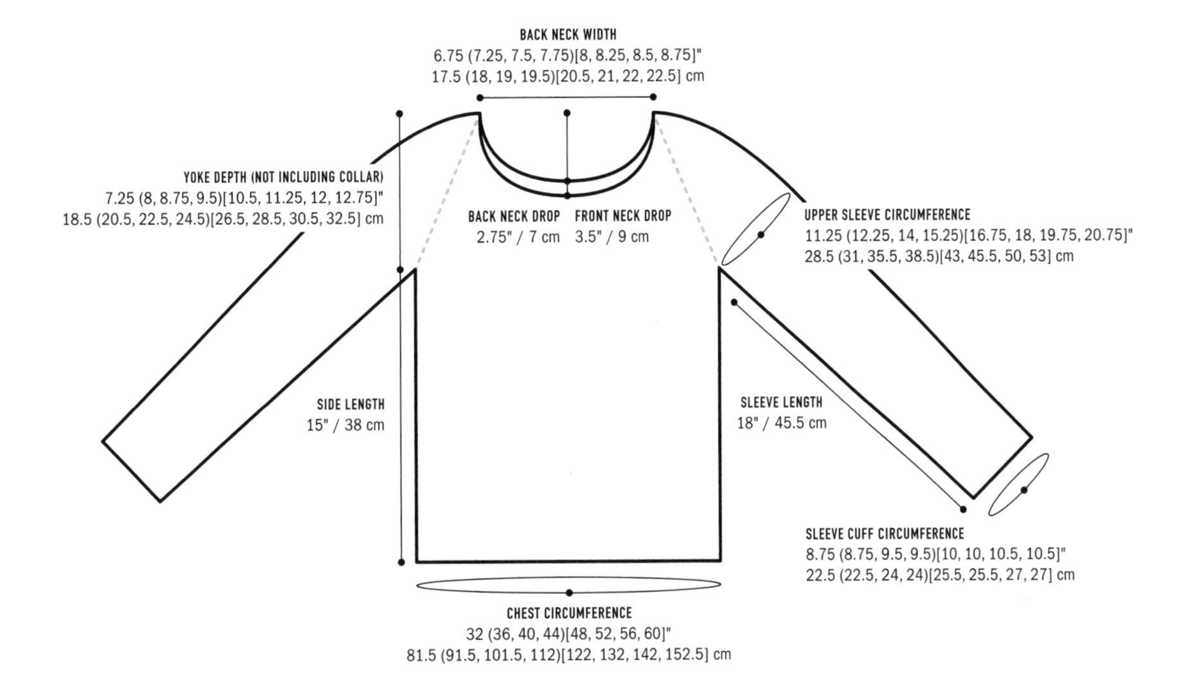

SLEEVES

Divide 35 (37, 41, 43)[47, 49, 53, 55] sleeve sts evenly over 3 larger dpns. With a 4th dpn pick up and knit 4 (6, 8, 10)[12, 14, 16, 18] sts from underarm edge and pm in the center of the picked up sts. Join for working in the rnd, knit to m. 39 (43, 49, 53)[59, 63, 69, 73] sts.

Cont in St st for 14 (11, 8, 6)[5, 4, 4, 3] rnds.

DEC RND: K1, ssk, knit to last 3 sts, k2tog, k1. 2 sts dec.

Rep this dec rnd every 15 (12, 9, 7)[6, 5, 5, 4] rnds 3 (3, 5, 9)[9, 13, 5, 15] times more, then every 0 (11, 8, 0)[5, 0, 4, 3] rnds 0 (2, 2, 0)[2, 0, 10, 2] times more. 31 (31, 33, 33)[35, 35, 37, 37] sts.

Cont in St st until sleeve meas 15" / 38 cm or 3" / 7.5 cm shorter than desired length.

DEC RND: K1, ssk, knit to end of rnd. 30 (30, 32, 32)[34, 34, 36, 36] sts.

Switch to smaller dpns.

RIBBING SETUP RND: (K1, p1) rep to end of rnd.

Cont in ribbing as est for 3" / 7.5 cm.

BO all sts in ribbing.

FINISHING

Weave in all ends. Block to measurements.

KNIT IN PIECES AND SEAMED

BACK

With smaller circular needle and using the long-tail cast on, CO 58 (64, 72, 78)[86, 92, 100, 106] sts.

RIBBING SETUP ROW (WS): (K1, p1) rep to end.

Rep this row until piece meas 3" / 7.5 cm from CO edge, inc 0 (1, 0, 1)[0, 1, 0, 1] st on last row. 58 (65, 72, 79)[86, 93, 100, 107] sts.

Switch to larger circular needle.

Cont working in St st until body meas 15" / 38 cm from CO edge, ending with a WS row.

SHAPE RAGLAN

BO 2 (3, 4, 5)[6, 7, 8, 9] sts at beg of next 2 rows. 54 (59, 64, 69)[74, 79, 84, 89] sts.

DEC ROW (RS): K2, ssk, knit to last 4 sts, k2tog, k2. 2 sts dec.

Rep this dec row every RS row 11 (13, 15, 17)[19, 21, 23, 25] times more, then every 4th row twice more. 26 (27, 28, 29)[30, 31, 32, 33] sts.

Work 5 rows even.

BO all sts.

FRONT

With smaller circular needle and using the long-tail cast on, CO 58 (64, 72, 78)[86, 92, 100, 106] sts.

RIBBING SETUP ROW (WS): (K1, p1) rep to end.

Rep this row until piece meas 3" / 7.5 cm from CO edge, inc 0 (1, 0, 1)[0, 1, 0, 1] st on last row. 58 (65, 72, 79)[86, 93, 100, 107] sts.

Switch to larger circular needle.

Cont working in St st until body meas 15" / 38 cm from CO edge, ending with a WS row.

SHAPE RAGLAN

BO 2 (3, 4, 5)[6, 7, 8, 9] sts at beg of next 2 rows. 54 (59, 64, 69)[74, 79, 84, 89] sts.

DEC ROW (RS): K2, ssk, knit to last 4 sts, k2tog, k2. 2 sts dec.

Rep this dec row every RS row 11 (13, 15, 17)[19, 21, 23, 25] times more, then every 4th row twice more. 26 (27, 28, 29)[30, 31, 32, 33] sts.

Purl 1 WS row.

(RS): K6, BO 14 (15, 16, 17)[18, 19, 20, 21] sts, knit to end. 6 sts each side.

SHAPE RIGHT NECK

Purl 1 WS row.

BO 2 sts, knit to end. 4 sts.

Purl 1 WS row.

BO all sts.

SHAPE LEFT NECK

Return to left front edge, ready to work a RS row.

Knit 1 RS row.

BO 2 sts, purl to end. 4 sts.

Knit 1 RS row.

BO all sts.

SLEEVE

With smaller circular needle and using the long-tail cast on, CO 33 (33, 35, 35)[37, 37, 39, 39] sts.

RIBBING SETUP ROW (WS): (P1, k1) rep to last st, p1.

Cont in ribbing as est until piece meas 3" / 7.5 cm from CO edge.

Switch to larger circular needle.

INC ROW (RS): K2, M1L, knit to 2 sts from end, M1R, k2. 2 sts inc.

Cont in St st, rep this inc row every 15 (11, 8, 7)[5, 5, 4, 3] rnds 3 (2, 2, 9)[2, 13, 10, 2] times more, then every 0 (12, 9, 0)[6, 0, 5, 4] rnds 0 (3, 5, 0)[9, 0, 5, 15] times more. 41 (45, 51, 55)[61, 65, 71, 75] sts.

Work even until sleeve meas 18" / 45.5 cm from CO edge, ending with a WS row.

SHAPE RAGLAN

BO 2 (3, 4, 5)[6, 7, 8, 9] sts at beg of next 2 rows. 37 (39, 43, 45)[49, 51, 55, 57] sts.

Work 2 rows even.

DEC ROW (RS): K2, ssk, knit to last 4 sts, k2tog, k2. 2 sts dec.

Rep this dec row every 4th row 5 (6, 6, 7)[7, 8, 8, 9] times more, every RS row 0 (0, 2, 2)[4, 4, 6, 6] times more, then every 4th row 2 times more. 21 sts.

Work 5 rows even.

BO all sts.

FINISHING

Seam raglan seams. Seam side and sleeve seams.

COLLAR

With smaller shorter circular needle, pick up and knit 1 st for every st along neck edge. 86 (88, 90, 92)[94, 96, 98, 100] sts.

Join for working in the rnd, being careful to not twist sts and pm to mark beg of rnd.

RIBBING SETUP RND: (K1, p1) rep to end.

Cont in ribbing as est for 7 rnds more.

BO all sts in ribbing.

Weave in all ends. Block to measurements.

TECHNIQUES

VIDEO TUTORIALS for some techniques are available at knitbot.com, including the following:

CAST ON METHODS

Backward loop cast on
Long-tail cast on

INCREASES

Make 1 left-slanting stitch (M1L): Make one stitch by lifting the bar between stitches from front to back with the left needle. Knit through the back of it with the right needle.

Make 1 right-slanting stitch (M1R): Make one stitch by lifting the bar between stitches from back to front with the left needle. Knit through the front of the stitch with the right needle.

DECREASES

Slip, slip, knit (ssk): To work this right-slanting decrease, slip the first stitch as if to knit, slip the second stitch as if to knit, then slide the left needle into the front part of both stitches and knit them together.

Knit 2 together (k2tog): To work this left-slanting decrease, knit two stitches together.

SHORT ROW SHAPING

Wrap and turn (w&t)
RS facing: With yarn in front, slip the next stitch knitwise from the left to the right needle. Move yarn to back. Slip stitch back from the right to the left needle. Turn work. One stitch has been wrapped.
WS facing: With yarn in back, slip the next stitch purlwise from the left to the right needle. Move yarn to front. Slip stitch back from the right to the left needle. One stitch has been wrapped.

ABBREVIATIONS

NEED MORE HELP WITH TECHNIQUES?

Your local yarn shop (LYS) can be a great resource not only for supplies but for classes and general knitting help.

A good A-to-Z how-to-knit book is a great investment for your library. There are many out there to choose from; here are a few I fancy:

Knitting for Dummies (Wiley, 2002)

Vogue Knitting: The Ultimate Knitting Book (Sixth & Spring, 2002)

Stitch 'n Bitch: The Knitter's Handbook (Workman Publishing, 2004)

The Principles of Knitting (Touchstone, 2012)

beg: beginning

BO: bind off

CO: cast on

cont: continue(s)(ing)

dec: decrease(d)(s)(ing)

dpn(s): double-pointed needle(s)

EOR: every other row / round

est: established

garter stitch: Knit all rows when working flat. Alternate knit 1 round, purl 1 round when working in the round.

inc: increase(d)(s)(ing)

k: knit

k2tog: knit two stitches togetherm**: marker**

M1L: make one left increase. See Techniques.

M1R: make one right increase. See Techniques.

meas: measure(s)(ing)

p: purl

p2tog: purl two stitches together

patt(s): pattern(s)

pm: place marker

rem(s): remain(s)(ing)

rep(s): repeat(s)

RS: Right Side

sm: slip marker

ssk: slip, slip, knit

ssp: slip, slip, purl

St st: Stockinette stitch. Knit on the right side, purl on the wrong side. When working in the round, knit all rounds.

st(s): stitch(es)

w&t: wrap and turn. See Techniques.

WS: Wrong Side

CREDITS

A special thank you to my ever supportive husband, Abe.

Thank you to Sam and Ruth Francis for allowing us to shoot at their beautiful home in Georgetown, Maine. If you fall in love with the location when looking through this book, you can rent your own cottage at Back River Bend!

Photography: Daniel Hudson
Graphic Design: Mary Joy Gumayagay
Technical Edit: Tana Pageler

Model: Lesley DeSantis
Hair and Makeup: Amy Valente
Prop Master: Rebekah Barter
Props: Fringe Supply Co.
Assistant: Aimee Chapman

Maine Map (page 57): Matt Barter